first love

Titles in the Seedbed Daily Text series:

The
Seedbed
Daily Text

first love

Philippians

J. D. WALT

Cover and page design by Strange Last Name
Page layout by PerfecType, Nashville, Tennessee

Walt, J. D. (John David)
    First love : Philippians / J.D. Walt. – Franklin, Tennessee : Seedbed Publishing, ©2021.

    pages ; cm. – (The Seedbed daily text)

    ISBN 9781628247992 (paperback)
    ISBN 9781628248005 (Mobi)
    ISBN 9781628248012 (ePub)
    ISBN 9781628248029 (uPDF)
    OCLC 1239996080

    1. Bible. Philippians--Meditations. 2. Spiritual exercises. I. Title. II. Series.

BS2705.45.W34 2021   242/.2   2021933534

SEEDBED PUBLISHING
Franklin, Tennessee
seedbed.com

Contents

An Invitation to Awakening

This resource comes with an invitation.

The invitation is as simple as it is comprehensive. It is not an invitation to commit your life to this or that cause or to join an organization or to purchase another book. The invitation is this: to wake up to the life you always hoped was possible and the reason you were put on planet Earth.

It begins with following Jesus Christ. In case you are unaware, Jesus was born in the first century BCE into a poor family from Nazareth, a small village located in what is modern-day Israel. While his birth was associated with extraordinary phenomena, we know little about his childhood. At approximately thirty years of age, Jesus began a public mission of preaching, teaching, and healing throughout the region known as Galilee. His mission was characterized by miraculous signs and wonders; extravagant care of the poor and marginalized; and multiple unconventional claims about his own identity and purpose. In short, he claimed to be the incarnate Son of God with the mission and power to save people from sin, deliver them from death, and bring them into the now and eternal kingdom of God—on earth as it is in heaven.

In the spring of his thirty-third year, during the Jewish Passover celebration, Jesus was arrested by the religious authorities, put on trial in the middle of the night, and at their urging, sentenced to death by a Roman governor. On the day known to history as Good Friday, Jesus was crucified on a Roman cross. He was buried in a borrowed tomb. On the following Sunday, according to multiple eyewitness accounts, he was physically raised from the dead. He appeared to hundreds of people, taught his disciples, and prepared for what was to come.

Forty days after the resurrection, Jesus ascended bodily into the heavens where, according to the Bible, he sits at the right hand of God, as the Lord of heaven and earth. Ten days after his ascension, in a gathering of more than three thousand people on the day of Pentecost, a Jewish day of celebration, something truly extraordinary happened. A loud and powerful wind swept over the people gathered. Pillars of what appeared to be fire descended upon the followers of Jesus. The Holy Spirit, the presence and power of God, filled the people, and the church was born. After this, the followers of Jesus went forth and began to do the very things Jesus did—preaching, teaching, and healing—planting churches and making disciples all over the world. Today, more than two thousand years later, the movement has reached us. This is the Great Awakening and it has never stopped.

Yes, two thousand years hence and more than two billion followers of Jesus later, this awakening movement of Jesus Christ and his church stands stronger than ever. Billions of ordinary people the world over have discovered in Jesus Christ an awakened life they never imagined possible. They have overcome challenges, defeated addictions, endured untenable hardships and suffering with unexplainable joy, and stared death in the face with the joyful confidence of eternal life. They have healed the sick, gathered the outcasts, embraced the oppressed, loved the poor, contended for justice, labored for peace, cared for the dying, and, yes, even raised the dead.

We all face many challenges and problems. They are deeply personal, yet when joined together, they create enormous and complex chaos in the world, from our hearts to our homes to our churches and our cities. All of this chaos traces to two originating problems: sin and death. Sin, far beyond mere moral failure, describes the fundamental broken condition of every human being. Sin separates us from God and others, distorts and destroys our deepest identity as the image-bearers of God, and poses a fatal problem from which we cannot save ourselves. It results in an ever-diminishing quality of life and ultimately ends in eternal death. Because Jesus lived a life of sinless perfection, he is able to save us from sin and restore us to a right relationship with God, others, and ourselves. He did this through his sacrificial death on the cross on our behalf. Because Jesus rose from the dead, he is able to deliver us from death and bring us into a quality of life both eternal and unending.

This is the gospel of Jesus Christ: pardon from the penalty of sin, freedom from the power of sin, deliverance from the grip of death, and awakening to the supernatural empowerment of the Holy Spirit to live powerfully for the good of others and the glory of God. Jesus asks only that we acknowledge our broken selves as failed sinners, trust him as our Savior, and follow him as our Lord. Following Jesus does not mean an easy life; however, it does lead to a life of power and purpose, joy in the face of suffering, and profound, even world-changing, love for God and people.

All of this is admittedly a lot to take in. Remember, this is an invitation. Will you follow Jesus? Don't let the failings of his followers deter you. Come and see for yourself.

Here's a prayer to get you started:

> Our Father in heaven, it's me (say your name), I want to know you. I want to live an awakened life. I confess I am a sinner. I have failed myself, others, and you in many ways. I know you made me for a purpose and I want to fulfill that purpose with my one life. I want to follow Jesus Christ. Jesus, thank you for the gift of your life and death and resurrection and ascension on my behalf. I want to walk in relationship with you as Savior and Lord. Would you lead me into the fullness and newness of life I was made for? I am ready to follow you. Come, Holy Spirit, and fill me with the love, power, and purposes of God. I pray these things by faith in the name of Jesus, amen.

It would be our privilege to help you get started and grow deeper in this awakened life of following Jesus. For some next steps and encouragements visit seedbed.com/awaken.

How the Daily Text Works

It seems obvious to say, but the Daily Text is written every day. Mostly it is written the day before it is scheduled to release online.

Before you read further, you are cordially invited to subscribe to and receive the daily e-mail. Visit seedbed.com /dailytext to get started. Also, check out the popular Facebook group, Seedbed Daily Text.

Eventually, the daily postings become part of a Daily Text discipleship resource. That's what you hold in your hands now.

It's not exactly a Bible study, though the Bible is both the source and subject. You will learn something about the Bible along the way: its history, context, original languages, and authors. The goal is not educational in nature but transformational. Seedbed is more interested in folks knowing Jesus than knowing *about* Jesus.

To that end, each reading begins with the definitive inspiration of the Holy Spirit, the ongoing, unfolding text of Scripture. Following that is a short and, hopefully, substantive insight from the text and some aspect of its meaning. For insight to lead to deeper influence, we turn the text into prayer. Finally, influence must run its course toward impact. This is why we ask each other questions. These questions are not designed to elicit information but to crystallize intention.

Discipleship always leads from inspiration to intention and from attention to action.

Using the Daily Text as a Discipleship Curricular Resource for Groups

While Scripture always addresses us personally, it is not written to us individually. The content of Scripture cries out for a community to address. The Daily Text is made for discipleship in community. This resource can work in several different ways. It could be read like a traditional book, a few pages or chapters at a time. Though unadvisable, the readings could be crammed in on the night before the meeting. Keep in mind, the Daily Text is not called the Daily Text for kicks. We believe Scripture is worthy of our most focused and consistent attention. Every day. We all have misses, but let's make every day more than a noble aspiration. Let's make it our covenant with one another.

For Use with Bands

In our judgment, the best and highest use of the Daily Text is made through what we call banded discipleship. A band is a same-gender group of three to five people who read together, pray together, and meet together to become the love of God for one another and the world. With banded discipleship, the daily readings serve more as a common text for the band and grist for the interpersonal conversation mill between meetings. The band meeting is reserved for the specialized activities of high-bar discipleship.

To learn more about bands and banded discipleship, visit discipleshipbands.com. Be sure to download the free *Discipleship Bands: A Practical Field Guide* or order a supply of the printed booklets online. Also be sure to explore Discipleship Bands, our native app designed specifically for the practice of banded discipleship, available in the App Store or Google Play.

For Use with Classes and Small Groups

The Daily Text has also proven to be a helpful discipleship resource for a variety of small groups, from community groups to Sunday school classes. Here are some suggested guidelines for deploying the Daily Text as a resource for a small group or class setting:

1. Hearing the Text

Invite the group to settle into silence for a period of no less than one and no more than five minutes. Ask an appointed person to keep time and to read the biblical text covering the period of days since the last group meeting. Allow at least one minute of silence following the reading of the text.

2. Responding to the Text

Invite anyone from the group to respond to the reading by answering these prompts: What did you hear? What did you see? What did you otherwise sense from the Lord?

3. Sharing Insights and Implications for Discipleship

Moving in an orderly rotation (or free-for-all), invite people to share insights and implications from the week's readings.

What did you find challenging, encouraging, provocative, comforting, invasive, inspiring, corrective, affirming, guiding, or warning? Allow group conversation to proceed at will. Limit to one sharing item per turn, with multiple rounds of discussion.

4. Shaping Intentions for Prayer

Invite each person in the group to share a single discipleship intention for the week ahead. It is helpful if the intention can also be framed as a question the group can use to check in from the prior week. At each person's turn, he or she is invited to share how their intention went during the previous week. The class or group can open and close their meeting according to their established patterns.

Introduction

No truer, more poignant, or more aspirationally ambitious words have ever been spoken than these from the tenth and eleventh verses of the third chapter of Paul's letter to the church in Philippi: "I want to know Christ and the power of his resurrection and the fellowship of sharing in his sufferings, becoming like him in his death, and so somehow, to attain to the resurrection from the dead" (NIV 1984).

This is our first love. To this we must return again and again and again. The whole genome of the Christian faith lives in these powerful words.

I want to know Christ. Let those words settle over you.

I want to know Christ. Let them lodge in your deepest heart.

I want to know Christ. This is our first love.

This is what it means to follow Jesus, to be a Christian. No matter how far along you are on the journey, no matter if you serve in the church vocationally or professionally— in fact, especially if you serve in the church vocationally or professionally—you never progress beyond this core aspiration: *I want to know Christ.*

In a wedding ceremony, the first act of worship is the declaration of intent by the bride and the groom. The parties are asked questions something like this these:

Do you take this man/woman to be your lawfully wedded spouse? Will you love him/her, comfort him/her, honor and keep him/her in sickness and in health, and forsaking all others keep only to him/her so long as you both shall live?

This is the kind of intent Jesus looks for in his followers.

I want to know Christ, and the power of his resurrection, and the fellowship of sharing in his sufferings, becoming like him in his death, and so somehow, to attain to the resurrection from the dead.

It can take time to get there, and be even more challenging to stay there, but this is the invitation. So why would we make such a declaration? Only one reason—Jesus has already made this kind of declaration toward us.

I want to know Christ.

If you are anything like me, though, I don't tend to linger too long there. I am eager to get to the next part of the declaration.

I want to know the power of his resurrection.

If I'm honest, that's what I'm most interested in. I want to know the resurrection power. I want to do the stuff Jesus did. I want to do great things in his name. I want to know the power of his resurrection.

But can we just pause and back up a step? We need to do more than linger with those first words. We must make camp there, and not just a temporary retreat kind of camp but a permanent camp. This is our home. First love.

I want to know Christ. Full stop.

Why is this so important? For starters, because if we ever get past it, we've lost it. There is no resurrection power outside of knowing Jesus. It is the fruit of the fellowship. And speaking of fellowship, watch where the text goes.

I want to know the fellowship of sharing in his sufferings.

Keeping it real here, I am not entirely sure I want to know this—the fellowship of sharing in his sufferings. You too? That's okay. This is a marathon we are running here, not a hundred-yard dash. Let's back up a couple of steps.

I want to know Christ, and the power of his resurrection . . .

So what if the point of the power of his resurrection is to enable us to participate in the fellowship of sharing in his sufferings? And what if within the fellowship of sharing in his sufferings is where the power of his resurrection becomes the most real and the most powerful? And what if this is where we really get to know Jesus? It gets deeper still.

. . . becoming like him in his death.

Okay, that's a bridge too far. But isn't this the very song Paul sings out in the second chapter of this letter—about having the same mind in us that was in Christ Jesus, who took on the nature of a slave, humbled himself, and became obedient to death, even death on a cross? Yes, Paul actually wants us to sing along with our lives.

This is moving past a declaration of intent and into something akin to vows. "For better or worse, for richer or poorer, in sickness and health, to love and to cherish, till death us do part." Only this is not till death do us part. Keep tracking.

I want to somehow attain to the resurrection of the dead.

While death is the end of a marriage, it looks to be the beginning of the life hid with Christ in God. The resurrection of the dead was a given for Paul. He said as much in his letter to the Corinthians. If the dead are not raised, then Christ was not raised. Permit me to ponder with you here. The resurrection of the dead was as fixed as the sun in Paul's understanding. He wasn't striving to attain that which was a given at the end of time. Paul believed there was an ever-increasing sense that though he would be raised on the last day, this future reality was available even now—in life—before death. Because Jesus had attained to the resurrection of the dead, in this life, Paul believed it was somehow possible for him—and us—to attain it now. It's why he wrote things in this letter like, "For to me, to live is Christ and to die is gain" (Phil. 1:21).

It gets richer. Here's the even deeper mystery. Paul has accelerated his own death, allowing it to become subsumed in the death of Jesus, and thereby abandoning his whole life to him. Consider how he put it in Galatians, "I have been crucified with Christ and I no longer live, but Christ lives in me. The life I now live in the body, I live by faith in the Son of God, who loved me and gave himself for me" (2:20).

And did I mention Paul wrote this letter from his retreat home overlooking the Mediterranean Ocean? No! Paul wrote this from a dank, dark prison cell. From a hopeless, joyless, and loveless place, Paul wrote what has become known as the Epistle of Joy. The one in greatest apparent need of encouragement became the greatest encourager of all time.

What was his secret? For Paul there was only ever this: I want to know Christ.

To know Jesus is to know everything else.

The power of his resurrection.

The fellowship of sharing in his sufferings.

The becoming like him in his death.

The somehow to attain to the resurrection from the dead.

It seems right and good to close out this introduction with perhaps Paul's greatest benediction, coming on the heels of the powerful declaration of his intention.

> Not that I have already obtained all this, or have already arrived at my goal, but I press on to take hold of that for which Christ Jesus took hold of me. Brothers and sisters, I do not consider myself yet to have taken hold of it. But one thing I do: Forgetting what is behind and straining toward what is ahead, I press on toward the goal to win the prize for which God has called me heavenward in Christ Jesus. (Phil. 3:12–14)

I want to know Christ. First love.

first love

Do You Have a Friend in the Gospel?

PHILIPPIANS 1:1A | Paul and Timothy, servants of Christ Jesus,

Consider This

"Paul and Timothy"? What's the meaning of this? Who does this? Who writes a letter from multiple senders? The answer: no one. In ancient letter-writing literature, this practice was unheard of. On this point, Paul is in his own category, and he did it in no less than seven of his letters.

Why Paul? Permit me the liberty of answering in my best impersonation of Paul.

Why "Paul and Timothy," you ask? It's because there is no *I* in *gospel*. The gospel is relationship. It is the relationship between Father, Son, and Holy Spirit. The gospel is not about me or about you. It is about us. Because the gospel is about love, it must be about relationship, for love cannot exist outside of a relationship.

This letter will be all about Paul's relationship with the Christians in Philippi. In fact, this letter will be a celebration of their friendship in the gospel. It is only fitting that the letter be birthed out of the relationship between Paul and Timothy.

The older I get, the more I understand that God doesn't use us as individuals. He indwells our relationships. Jesus looks for two or three gathered in his name (Matt. 18:20). He says people will know we follow him by the way we love each other (John 13:35). He attaches the very success of the gospel to the quality of our relationships and their embeddedness in his relationship with the Father. When he teaches us to pray, he says to say, "Our Father" (Matt. 6:9). Even in the hiddenness of our personal prayer closet we say, "Our."

As Americans we tend to fundamentally misunderstand the nature of a personal relationship with God. We equate personal with individual and individual with private. Our relationship with God is intimately personal, but it is not private. Our relationship with God is uniquely individual but never isolated. It is personal and corporate. It is individual and communal. It is Paul and Timothy.

Perhaps this is our big impediment to actually sharing the gospel. We think the gospel is a body of content that one person must share with another person. What if the gospel is more about the sharing of a radically open relationship with an ever-widening circle of would-be friends? What if it's not me who shares the gospel, but we?

What might it look like to find and found our friendships in the gospel?

The Prayer

Abba Father, we thank you for your Son, Jesus, who calls us his friends. Teach us the way of founding and finding our friendships in the gospel. Show us the way of consecrating our friendships for your purposes in the world and give us the joy of seeing you bear fruit through them, and all of this for your glory. We pray in Jesus' name, amen.

The Questions

- How does this challenge your sense of relationship with God? Do you have a "me and Jesus" mentality?
- What would it look like to have a "we and Jesus" mindset? How can your friendships become leveraged by the gospel of Jesus?
- Like Paul and Timothy, who comes after your "and"? Who is your friend in the gospel?

Why Small Is the New Large

2

PHILIPPIANS 1:1B | To all God's holy people in Christ Jesus at Philippi, together with the overseers and deacons:

Consider This

I fear we have the wrong picture in our minds when we think of the church at Philippi. I mean, for this place to be one of only several churches in all of the world to merit a letter from the apostle Paul (and Timothy), and for this letter to not only survive until the present day but to be canonized as Holy Scripture—it had to be something amazing. Didn't it?

I think it's fair to estimate when Paul writes, "To all God's holy people in Christ Jesus at Philippi, together with the overseers and deacons," he's talking to what would be a pretty small church in our way of sizing things up. When he first arrived, there weren't even enough Jewish men (ten) to field a team. They had no synagogue. Paul had to walk a mile outside of the city to a nearby river to even find a prayer meeting. Ten years later they had grown into a full-fledged church. But in our way of thinking of church plants and church growth, these guys would still be in the school gymnasium phase.

We probably wouldn't consider them too successful by our standards. But what if we have the wrong standards? We so want to measure our churches and their impact by the ABCs: attendance, buildings, and cash. Paul wants the gospel to spread, but he will not be seduced by numbers or deceived by appearances. Paul has one metric for the growth of the church and the spread of the gospel. It's not the number of people that matters to Paul but the holiness of the people.

To all God's holy people in Christ Jesus at Philippi, together with the overseers and deacons:

The Greek word for "holy" is *hagios*, and it means something like special, different, distinctive, unlike the prevailing surrounding culture, or in the midst of yet set apart. And let's be clear. The last thing Paul is interested in doing is setting up little clubs of holier-than-thou legalists who measure each other's performance by their religious activity and who judge the outside world according to their pagan proclivities.

Holiness used to mean something like strictly rigorous religious observance for Paul. That all changed the day he was knocked off his proverbial high horse. Now holiness means something altogether different. Holiness means one thing and one thing alone: the holy love of God made known through the risen Lord Jesus Christ in the power of the Holy Spirit.

To all God's holy people in Christ Jesus at Philippi, together with the overseers and deacons:

What if we began to measure our faith and the faith of our local church communities according to the metrics of the New Testament as laid out in this letter? It would probably become a lot less about last Sunday's attendance and next year's building project and a lot more about cultivating a holy obsession with becoming a holy people and what that really means (and what it doesn't).

In the coming days and decades, I suspect the real church is going to look a lot more like a half a dozen people quietly and powerfully travailing in prayer down by the river than the massive building project on a hundred acres on the outskirts of town. And, please, don't take this as a rant against megachurches. I'm just saying if megachurches (or any churches, for that matter) want to count in the new-old world rising up around them, they must concern themselves a lot more with their micro dimensions.

One thing we can learn today from the little church in Philippi: where the holiness of Jesus is in play, small will be the new big.

The Prayer

Abba Father, we thank you for your Son, Jesus, who will make us as holy as we want to become by the power of your indwelling Spirit. Come, Holy Spirit, and increase our desire for Jesus' kind of holiness. It is in his name, we pray, amen.

The Questions

- One of the hard questions my mentor Maxie Dunnam is fond of asking is: "How deep is your desire for holiness?"
- What is the vision for a holy version of you? What is the caricature of that vision?
- What is holding you back from pursuing this vision? Will it be worth it?

3 | Christianity Is Not the Power of Positive Thinking

PHILIPPIANS 1:2 | Grace and peace to you from God our Father and the Lord Jesus Christ.

Consider This

For anyone who has been around church or reading the Bible for any length of time, greetings like this can seem so throwaway and even cliché:

Grace and peace to you from God our Father and the Lord Jesus Christ.

Honestly, these words strike me with no particular force or spiritual power. How about you? It's just the standard Sunday school salutation, isn't it?

It reminds me of that scene early in the story of *Charlotte's Web* when Charlotte, the spider, awakens Wilbur, the pig, by saying, "Salutations!"

When Paul writes, "Grace and peace to you from God our Father and the Lord Jesus Christ," it's not just a fancy way of saying hello. He's using the two power words of the Christian faith. Grace, or *karis* in Greek, means the unearned, undeserved, unmitigated favor of God. Peace, or *shalom* in Hebrew, means the unexplainable way God is putting the world back together again in the midst of all the unsettled chaos still spewing out.

Note that this is not Paul's optimism. Paul speaks for God. Grace and peace are not from Paul but *from God our Father and the Lord Jesus Christ.*

We should probably mention at this point that Paul is not writing a wispy postcard from somewhere on a beach. Paul is in a Roman prison. Grace and peace would seem to be the last thing on Paul's mind in the crap-storm that had become his life. Paul is not getting his zen on; he is not finding a transcendental meditative calm in the eye of the storm.

Often we think of our faith as though it were a positive perspective on things—a way of seeing life from another angle. The Christian faith is not a perspective. And it is certainly not the power of positive thinking (as helpful as that can be at times). It's a point of view, another concept I think we misappropriate. My point of view is not my opinion. It's the point or place from which I am seeing things. The Christian faith is not another human perspective on life. It is God's point of view. It sounds audacious to claim to have God's point of view, doesn't it? But is this not precisely what Scripture claims—to be God's point of view?

Grace and peace to you from God our Father and the Lord Jesus Christ.

Paul is not writing from a Christian perspective, he is writing from God's point of view. He is not trying to help us see things differently, as in "The glass is really half full." Paul boldly yet humbly declares the way God sees things. He will come to define this gifted and graced point of view with two words: "in Christ."

Stay tuned. That's where we're headed.

The Prayer

Abba Father, we thank you for your Son, Jesus, who reveals to us your point of view with perfection. Bring us into your point of view. Bring us into the mystery and power of a life "in Christ." We pray in Jesus' name, amen.

The Questions

- What do you think about this distinction I am drawing between a perspective on something and a point of view?
- We live in a world that wants to reduce the Christian faith to just another perspective among many others. What does it look like to claim God's point of view with humility?

Why Our Local Church Must Become like the Pittsburg Steelers Again

4

PHILIPPIANS 1:3–6 ESV | I thank my God in all my remembrance of you, always in every prayer of mine for you all making my prayer with joy, because of your partnership in the gospel from the first day until now. And I am sure of this, that he who began a good work in you will bring it to completion at the day of Jesus Christ.

Consider This

The little church in Philippi didn't have a street address, but they knew their station. Birthed in a dream, they didn't have a vision; they *were* a vision. Remember this? "During the night Paul had a vision of a man of Macedonia standing and begging him, 'Come over to Macedonia and help us.' After Paul had seen the vision, we got ready at once to leave for Macedonia, concluding that God had called us to preach the gospel to them" (Acts 16:9–10).

Named by Philip II, father of Alexander the Great, Philippi had its own storied past. It was the site of the most significant military engagement in all the Roman Empire. In 42 BC Mark Antony and Octavius conquered the republican forces of the assassins of Julius Caesar, Cassius, and Brutus. Philippi was the pride of the empire, a "little Rome" for which the empire had high hopes.

This is how it all began in Philippi. They were the first church in town. They were the first church in all of Europe! In one sense or another, this is how every church we see today began—as a dream, a vision, a small group of people who saw it and welcomed it from a distance, beckoning the horizon of the kingdom of God into their town.

When the people heard the letter and words like, "he who began a good work in you will bring it to completion at the day of Jesus Christ," they didn't hear it as so many isolated individuals searching for isolated, individual, self-fulfilling lives in the world. They heard it more like the Pittsburgh Steelers would hear a coach beckoning them toward the Super Bowl.

Somehow we've lost our sense of the local church as the Pittsburgh Steelers. We have lost the sense of our towns and cities as battlefields of darkness versus light and of death versus life. We have lost the sense of our fellowship (no matter how small or large) as the tip of the spear of the kingdom of God. What if we could see our churches that way again, as movements in our communities? To one degree or another, that's how every one of them began. What if we could begin again? Would you want to?

One of my favorite quotes is from C. S. Lewis's *Screwtape Letters*, a series of short letters written from the vantage point of a senior demon instructing a junior demon on how to effectively tempt people. This excerpt is from a letter concerning the church:

One of our great allies at present is the Church itself. Do not misunderstand me. I do not mean the Church as we see her spread out through all time and space and rooted in eternity, terrible as an army with banners. That, I confess, is a spectacle which makes our boldest tempters uneasy. But fortunately it is quite invisible to these humans.[*]

The Prayer

Abba Father, we thank you for your Son, Jesus, who would make all of our churches outposts of the kingdom of God against which the gates of hell will not prevail. Rekindle our sense of the church from your point of view. Awaken us to the possibilities of our church anew. We pray in Jesus' name, amen.

The Questions

- Pastors and leaders, you didn't answer a call to ministry in order to become a religious service provider, did you? So why did you do it?
- Church members, you didn't join the church to be a religious consumer using the goods of the church primarily to meet your own needs, did you? So why did you do it?

---

[*] C. S. Lewis, *The Screwtape Letters* (New York: HarperCollins, 2001), 5.

5

This May Be the Most Important Question I Will Ever Ask You

PHILIPPIANS 1:7–8 | It is right for me to feel this way about all of you, since I have you in my heart and, whether I am in chains or defending and confirming the gospel, all of you share in God's grace with me. God can testify how I long for all of you with the affection of Christ Jesus.

Consider This

Paul not only loved the Philippians, he liked them.

God can testify how I long for all of you with the affection of Christ Jesus.

It's been close to twenty years ago—I remember the day. I was pastoring the leaders of the biggest event I had ever been a part of (before or since). We gathered the evening before the event began for a time of consecration. As each of the leaders came forward, two or three of us would lay hands on them and pray prayers of blessing and consecration as they knelt to offer themselves for the Lord's service.

As the time came to a close, one of the men who had been helping with this work caught my eye. He approached and asked if he could pray for me. As he prayed he broke pace with his words and moved into a kind of prophesying, as though he were speaking words straight from the heart of God into my deepest self. I will never forget those words. He said, "John David, you know I love you, but I need you to know that I don't just love you. I like you. I want you to know that I like you."

That moment changed me. It was an awakening to the affection of God—not for the world—but for me. I have carried those words with me ever since. They changed the way I understood the nature of the love of God. They also changed the way I understood the nature of loving other people.

God can testify how I long for all of you with the affection of Christ Jesus.

So many people understand the love of God as a kind of divine tolerance for them. As a result, the world often understands the love of the church and its members as the selfsame kind of tolerance (or not) for them. Then, by the grace of God, a follower of Jesus comes along and gets close enough to you to see you. They don't see you through the lenses of their own brokenness or their idealism (which are often two sides of the same coin). They have a mysterious capacity to see you like God sees you. Their love takes the form of a deep like. They don't love you in spite of your brokenness or because of it. They like you just because of you.

These are the ones who know the affection of Christ Jesus for themselves. These are the ones who are learning to trust this affection so much so that they have learned to like themselves. And these are the ones who cause us to dare to believe something different about God and about ourselves.

I'm going to tell you now what I believe may be the deepest, perhaps the hardest (and as a consequence, most neglected) truth of the gospel. We tend to believe our love for others originates from God's love for us, and it does—just not how we think. Our love for others will never exceed our love for ourselves, and our love for ourselves will never exceed our awareness and experience of God's love for us. No one knew this better than Jesus, who put it this way: "And the second is like it: 'Love your neighbor as yourself'" (Matt. 22:39).

It's why, in John's gospel, Jesus brings the entire gospel down to a single command: "Love each other as I have loved you" (John 15:12).

We must know, beyond knowledge, God's love for us. In other words, you've got to know God likes you. This is the whole point of Jesus. This may be the most important question I will ever ask you: Do you know Jesus likes you?

As we go along, we will see just how deeply Paul understood this. His affection for others flowed like a river from his affection for himself, which flowed like a river from his experience of Jesus' affection for him. That's the mystery and the miracle of the gospel. We can settle for no less ourselves.

The Prayer

Abba Father, we thank you for your Son, Jesus, who likes us as much as he loves us. Fill us with this knowledge beyond mere acceptance of it. Make it our lives. We must know this, Lord. Come, Holy Spirit, and awaken us to this love in a way that all that holds us back can be pushed aside. We pray in Jesus' name, amen.

The Questions

- How do you relate to this idea of being liked by God and how that clarifies the nature of God's love for you?
- Do you like yourself? Why or why not?
- How is it that we can put all the focus on loving our neighbor and none of the focus on loving ourselves when Jesus so directly connects the two?

Does Love Matter like the Moon or the Sun?

6

PHILIPPIANS 1:9–11 | And this is my prayer: that your love may abound more and more in knowledge and depth of insight, so that you may be able to discern what is best and may be pure and blameless for the day of Christ, filled with the fruit of righteousness that comes through Jesus Christ—to the glory and praise of God.

Consider This

Over the years I have held many different conceptions and misconceptions of the Christian faith and what it is really about. First it was about good, moral training—telling the truth and refraining from stealing from my mother's purse and not killing my sisters and essential stuff like that. Then it became about going to heaven and not going to hell and making sure I had the software agreement with Jesus right.

Then it shifted to making sure I showed up for church and kept my life between the ditches. Next came self-improvement and living a fulfilling life. After that came an awakening to a call to serve the church, and growing the church became the thing. At fifty, I think I may be finally coming to the heart of it all. Paul's prayer in today's text clarifies it for us:

And this is my prayer: that your love may abound more and more in knowledge and depth of insight, so that you may be able to discern what is best and may be pure and blameless for the day of Christ, filled with the fruit of righteousness that comes through Jesus Christ—to the glory and praise of God.

Maybe it was necessary to go through all these stages and phases. I wonder, though, what if someone had taught me this from the start—that it was about love, not the flimsy cultural construct that gets passed off as love but the supernatural reality of the truth and power of God that alone changes people and situations?

Love was always there, kind of like the moon—something you see and believe but otherwise salute as an amazing ideal. You always knew the moon mattered and people had been there but that was about it. Like going to the moon, you always knew it was possible to become a person of love, just not practical. I knew I would never go there because even though it was possible, it would not be possible for me. My notion of the love of God would be like my relationship with the moon. I would always know it was there, and from time to time I would notice it and at other times even gaze upon it, but otherwise I would need to focus my energies on revolving around the sun, which felt more like making a living and raising a family and all the other things one does to make a life. The moon would revolve around me while I revolved around the sun.

If there is one thing I have learned and continue to learn and will need to relearn every day for the rest of my life, it is this: love is the sun. The love of God in Jesus Christ is the white-hot, blazing sun of all reality. No sun means no light. No sun means no life. No sun means no order. Just as everything must revolve around the sun, everything must revolve around the love of God. It is the only power. It is the organizing center. It is the core principle of all order. The love of God in Jesus Christ is the light of the world. It is the life of the world. Until we understand this, all of life, work, faith, religion, and church will exist in some semblance of managed chaos.

Grasping this and all its myriad and miraculous implications is the very essence of Paul's prayer.

And this is my prayer: that your love may abound more and more in knowledge and depth of insight, so that you may be able to discern what is best and may be pure and blameless for the day of Christ, filled with the fruit of righteousness that comes through Jesus Christ—to the glory and praise of God.

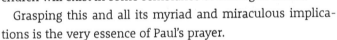

Love is the center and the circumference. Love is the means and the end, the lock and the key. I see this opening prayer as the governing dynamic of the whole letter. Paul will try to explain it, but it can only be revealed to someone. This is why Paul prays. And it's why we must pray our way through it with him. Come, Holy Spirit!

The Prayer

And this is our prayer: that our love may abound more and more in knowledge and depth of insight, so that you and I will be able to discern what is best and may be pure and blameless for the day of Christ, filled with the fruit of righteousness that comes through Jesus Christ—to the glory and praise of God. In Jesus' name we pray, amen.

The Questions

- Has the love of God been more like the moon for you or is it becoming the sun?
- Do you think we must pass through all these approximations of what the Christian faith is all about or could we get to the heart of the matter much earlier in our journey? Reflect on that.
- If it is not about love, what is it about?

7 The Surprising Sophistication of the Gospel in Suffering

PHILIPPIANS 1:12–14 | Now I want you to know, brothers and sisters, that what has happened to me has actually served to advance the gospel. As a result, it has become clear throughout the whole palace guard and to everyone else that

I am in chains for Christ. And because of my chains, most of the brothers and sisters have become confident in the Lord and dare all the more to proclaim the gospel without fear.

Consider This

Now that the salutations are over, Paul gets to the bad news. Everyone had been talking about Paul's situation. Things were just getting off the ground; the Holy Spirit was moving profoundly in large cities through these tiny churches. The apostolic dream was happening, but the apostle was in jail.

We read it so matter-of-factly and with such familiarity today that we miss its gravity. Paul had given everything to Jesus. How could this be happening to him? He did everything he was asked to do, and this was his reward—a Roman prison cell? Surely this wasn't God's idea for a new recruitment strategy for young preachers. If the gospel was such good news, why was its leader facing such bad news? This was not just another day at the office for the young New Testament church. This was catastrophic.

Consider Paul's words: "Now I want you to know, brothers and sisters, that what has happened to me has actually served to advance the gospel."

Translation: You can put the apostle in jail, but you can't imprison the gospel. It will only get stronger. We so want the Christian faith to be a "get out of jail free" card, immunity from tragedy, protection from terminal cancer, and a happy life in the suburbs. It is none of those things. Instead, following Jesus should more often take us into harm's way than out of it. Why? It's in the most turbulent storms where Jesus demonstrates the most transformational suffering. These are the places where the awful things that happen to us actually serve to advance the gospel.

Jail may sideline Paul for a couple of years, but it will only speed up the movement of the gospel:

As a result, it has become clear throughout the whole palace guard and to everyone else that I am in chains for Christ.

When you put Paul in jail, you put Jesus in jail, and when you put Jesus in jail, the jail changes. Give a tried-and-true follower of Jesus cancer and you give Jesus cancer, and when you give Jesus cancer, he will make cancer serve the purposes of God. This is what the gospel does. Jesus can take a situation far from the realm of God's purpose and cause it to serve the purposes of God in astonishing ways.

We must only allow our suffering to lead us to deeper surrender to Jesus. This means renouncing victimhood, releasing entitlement, and finding a posture of unshakable faith in Jesus rather than devoting all our energies to fighting against the circumstance. The truth? The circumstance may not change. The gospel? Everything else can. And, so often, it's the "everything else" that matters most. Isn't that what Paul says here?

And because of my chains, most of the brothers and sisters have become confident in the Lord and dare all the more to proclaim the gospel without fear.

Count on it. Every time and in every one of these situations, many are watching and waiting to see God arise. We all want a simple escape hatch. The gospel is far more sophisticated and surprising. Let's give them something to talk about.

The Prayer

Abba Father, we thank you for your Son, Jesus, who reveals to us what it looks like to take the most horrific suffering that was the cross and endure it to the other side of resurrection and the most honorific glory. Show us this way of the cross in our own lives and especially in our darkest hours. Come, Holy Spirit, and either deliver us from our suffering or deliver us more deeply into your possibilities in the midst of it. We pray in Jesus' name, amen.

The Questions

- Can you think of a situation where someone else's valiant faith in the face of hardship and suffering actually increased your own faith?
- How do you relate to the notion that an unfair hardship may not be God's purpose but can powerfully serve the purposes of God? Have you ever seen that in your own life?
- What difficult, devastating, or impossible situation might you be facing right now? Where are you in it? Blaming, resigning to the circumstance, or surrendering more deeply to Jesus?

8 How to Take the High Road in the Face of Insult

PHILIPPIANS 1:15–18A | It is true that some preach Christ out of envy and rivalry, but others out of goodwill. The latter do so out of love, knowing that I am put here for the defense of the gospel. The former preach Christ out of selfish ambition, not sincerely, supposing that they can stir up trouble for me while I am in chains. But what does it matter? The important thing is that in every way, whether from false motives or true, Christ is preached. And because of this I rejoice.

Consider This

Paul is in jail, and, if I'm reading it right, it sounds like some of the preachers back in Philippi are having a heyday with it. They are stirring up trouble. I suspect Paul's reputation is taking a severe hit. They are seizing the opportunity to kick him while he's down.

We don't mean to do this, but we all have a tendency toward it. We create false narratives based on incomplete and often inaccurate information, and we go with it. Here's how such a conversation might have gone:

> AVERAGE CHURCH MEMBER IN PHILIPPI: Did you hear the news? Paul is in prison in Rome.
>
> JEALOUS UNDERLING PREACHER: Yes, we heard. I feel bad for him, but it's becoming a pattern for him.

AVERAGE CHURCH MEMBER IN PHILIPPI: What do you mean? Some of us were wanting to take up a collection to help him.

JEALOUS UNDERLING PREACHER: I mean, don't you remember what happened right here in Philippi? He was thrown in jail and got Silas arrested too.

AVERAGE CHURCH MEMBER IN PHILIPPI: But don't you remember the way the church prayed for them and the miraculous way they were delivered from prison? I wasn't here then, but I've heard the amazing story.

JEALOUS UNDERLING PREACHER: Right. You mean the earthquake? And then Paul got all high-handed with them about arresting a Roman citizen. I will be honest—a lot of us were glad to see Paul go, and now he's back in jail and asking us for help. The guy's a troublemaker.

AVERAGE CHURCH MEMBER IN PHILIPPI: I guess I didn't realize all of that. I thought Paul was pretty loved around here.

JEALOUS UNDERLING PREACHER: Yes, isn't that how it always is—people hear what they want to hear. And, as for the money, there are so many needs right here in our backyard. How can we justify sending more money to a glorified ex-con? . . . I mean present con.

AVERAGE CHURCH MEMBER IN PHILIPPI: I hear what you are saying. We will see what happens.

Isn't that how it always happens?

So, how would you have responded in Paul's position? I may have said something like, "Are you kidding me? Do you believe a single word that jealous underling preacher has to say? Consider the source. He knows you all listen to me and wants me out. This is his chance. Just ask Epaphroditus. He will tell you the truth. You all should send this guy packing."

Paul had gotten word about this, but rather than entering the fray and taking on these jealous underling preacher types, he gave them the benefit of the doubt.

It is true that some preach Christ out of envy and rivalry . . . The former preach Christ out of selfish ambition, not sincerely, supposing that they can stir up trouble for me while I am in chains. But what does it matter? The important thing is that in every way, whether from false motives or true, Christ is preached. And because of this I rejoice.

That, my friends, is what you call a mature Christian response. Jesus wins, and because Jesus wins we may endure losses, but we will not lose. That's the secret sauce of a mature Christian disposition.

The Prayer

Lord Jesus, yours is the name that is above every name. We thank you that we bear your name, which means we can be truly humble. Help us when we are misrepresented or maligned to not take it personally but to instead take the high road. Grow us up into maturity, even the fullness of Christ. We pray in Jesus' name, amen.

The Questions

- Why do we have such a need to defend and vindicate ourselves when we are done wrong as Paul was in Philippi?
- How can we make a better response than the average church member in Philippi?
- What keeps us from taking the high road in such gossipy scenarios as this one?

The More Excellent Way of Prayer

9

PHILIPPIANS 1:18B–20 | Yes, and I will continue to rejoice, for I know that through your prayers and God's provision of the Spirit of Jesus Christ what has happened to me will turn out for my deliverance. I eagerly expect and hope that I will in no way be ashamed, but will have sufficient courage so that now as always Christ will be exalted in my body, whether by life or by death.

Consider This

Paul is in prison . . .

And Paul is rejoicing.

How can this be? If there is one place I cannot imagine rejoicing, it would be prison. Paul has so deeply and thoroughly surrendered his life to Jesus that though he is completely vulnerable to the schemes of men, he is totally invincible. You cannot kill the one who has already died. In this way, Paul blazes the trail that will be followed by every saint to follow who is worth their salt. He knows the secret to life—which is to die before you die. His ambitions and aspirations are dead and buried. Now his life can be consumed by a holy passion. Soon we will hear his mission statement: "To live is Christ and to die is gain" (v. 21).

How does one get to such a place? Paul gives us a hint:

I know that through your prayers and God's provision of the Spirit of Jesus Christ what has happened to me will turn out for my deliverance.

Sometimes when people say they are praying for you it means one thing, and other times it means something altogether different. If I'm honest, I easily fall into a working definition of prayer that locates me in the place of an intermediary. My prayers center on my care and concern for others and bringing this care and concern before God in the form of a request on their behalf. It's why when I (and I suspect many of you) say, "I'm praying for you," or, "I'll pray for you," it means I care and am concerned about you and I will mention that to God. It's a sentiment that goes about as deep as my own commitment to you. Prayer becomes about me passing on your need to God to stand with you and resolve your situation.

An intermediary serves as a link between one person and another. I don't think this is how Paul understands the Philippian believers' prayers for him.

There is a better way. The New Testament does not conceive of prayer as the work of an intermediary but as that of an intercessor. An intercessor actually intervenes and gets involved. An intermediary sees their task as asking God to stand with you. An intercessor understands their work as standing with God for you. When I stand with God for you, I begin to share in the burden of the love God has for you. I'm not just passing on a request as the middleman. When I intercede for you, my concern for you becomes infused with God's concern for you. I cease to be moved by my own best efforts. I no longer understand my own best efforts as some kind of strategy to get God to do something.

When I intercede, I open my will and my willingness to God in a way that wills the Holy Spirit–power-filled love of God into your life and situation. This is not about prayer changing me and me changing things. I do not become the answer to my own prayer. No, the intercessor enters into a mysterious way of participation with God in the process and in the answering. Intercession leads to the release of the power of God (which is love) in the world to work in new ways and to open up new possibilities that did not exist before.

This is why Paul counts so much on the prayers of the little Philippian church. Through the person and power of the Holy Spirit, they stand with God for Paul, and, as a consequence, despite their physical distance, they stand with Paul for the gospel.

This is why Paul always references his praying as a kind of travail. He speaks of it on one occasion as being in the pains of childbirth (Gal. 4:19). This is why down through the ages the saints speak of prayer not as preparation for the work but as the work itself.

The Prayer

Abba Father, we thank you for your Son, Jesus, who is our Great Intercessor and who calls us to share in this work with him for the sake of the whole world. Would you lead us in this way of prayer? We confess we hardly grasp it, but we believe. We are tired of casual prayer. We want to participate in this greater work. Come, Holy Spirit. In Jesus' name we pray, amen.

The Questions

- What do you think of this difference between an intermediary and an intercessor? Make sense? Where are you in that?
- Are you willing (or willing to be made willing) to become an intercessor in prayer? It's not something you can just decide and do; you must ask God to do it in and through you.
- Do you see the difference between your good-natured care and concern for another person and the burden of God's love for them?

If "To Die Is Gain," What's the Point of Staying Alive?

10

PHILIPPIANS 1:21–26 | For to me, to live is Christ and to die is gain. If I am to go on living in the body, this will mean fruitful labor for me. Yet what shall I choose? I do not know! I am torn between the two: I desire to depart and be with Christ, which is better by far; but it is more necessary for you that I remain in the body. Convinced of this, I know that I will remain, and I will continue with all of you for your progress and joy in the faith, so that through my being with you again your boasting in Christ Jesus will abound on account of me.

Consider This

My grandfather (a.k.a. "Peepaw") was fond of telling the well-known joke of the preacher standing up in church on Sunday morning and saying, "Everybody who wants to go to heaven, please stand up." All stood with the exception of one older man on the back row. The preacher asked, "Sir, don't you want to go to heaven?" He responded, "Yes, I want to go to heaven, just not on the first load."

Was it Loretta Lynn or B. B. King who first said, "Everybody wants to go to heaven, but nobody wants to die"?

Not Paul. On this he is clear: "For to me, to live is Christ and to die is gain." Paul is ready to take the first bus. He does not have a death wish; he has a profound vision of eternal life, which has clearly already begun for him but will go to one thousand times when his body expires. And let's be clear: Paul is not all about going to heaven when he dies. As we will see, his ultimate hope is for the resurrection of the body and the new creation, which far from somewhere up there, is decidedly down here.

The big point for Paul is Jesus only, Jesus ever: "For to me, to live is Christ and to die is gain." What I find most interesting is Paul's motivation for continuing in his present bodily existence. I think most people's primary motivation for staying alive—beyond their fear of death—is to enjoy life, to take more and better family vacations, to play more golf, and maybe win the lottery. Not Paul. Paul's interest in staying alive is to help other people. He wants to stay alive for the sake of the gospel of Jesus flourishing in the lives of people.

If I am to go on living in the body, this will mean fruitful labor for me. . . . Convinced of this, I know that I will remain, and I will continue with all of you for your progress and joy in the faith.

So, I'm asking myself these questions today: Do I really believe "to live is Christ"? Do I really believe "to die is gain"? If so, why do I want to remain alive in the body?

The Prayer

Abba Father, we thank you for your Son, Jesus, who is the way and the truth and the life. Search our hearts, O Lord, and help us answer the question: Is Christ our life, or is he just our help, or is he something less to us? Give us clarity on this.

We want Christ to be our all in all. Save us from the ease of self-deception on this point. We pray in Jesus' name, amen.

The Questions
- Do you really believe "to live is Christ"?
- Do you really believe "to die is gain"?
- If so, why do you want to remain alive in the body?

Why We Don't Live in America Anymore

11

PHILIPPIANS 1:27–28 | Whatever happens, conduct yourselves in a manner worthy of the gospel of Christ. Then, whether I come and see you or only hear about you in my absence, I will know that you stand firm in the one Spirit, striving together as one for the faith of the gospel without being frightened in any way by those who oppose you. This is a sign to them that they will be destroyed, but that you will be saved—and that by God.

Consider This
Whatever happens, conduct yourselves in a manner worthy of the gospel of Christ.

What do you hear when you hear Paul say this?

Do you know what I hear? I hear him say, "Behave!"

Why? Because I have grown up in an era of the church that has allowed the culture of the surrounding world to reduce the culture of the church to one of believing and behaving. I'm not saying this was the case in Philippi, just here and now.

The world understands the church primarily as a "don't" society, who lives according to a moral code (or doesn't, as the case may be). Further, the world understands the church to somehow expect the world to live by that same moral code, and when the world does not, the church acts surprised and judges them accordingly.

Attention, readers. We do not live in that America anymore. We live in Philippi (in a manner of speaking). We now live in an age where people do not define themselves by their sex but by their sexuality. And when it comes to one's sex, Facebook now offers somewhere upward of seventy different options for gender selection. Today there are more than one thousand casinos operating across our fifty states. Forty-four of our states have lotteries. This year we will see just shy of one million abortions. Within twenty years, marijuana will be legal in one form or another in every state.

And all of this is happening on our watch. The late, great, gospel prophet of country music Merle Haggard asked the question well: "Are we rolling downhill like a snowball headed for hell?" So what are we to do? Get mad at the world? Protest? Retreat and hide?

We do not live in that America anymore. We live in Philippi. Whatever that America was, it's not coming back anytime soon. In fact, we need to let it go. We must let go of

America's good old days and start to seek a better country—the kingdom of God. If we were missionaries to Philippi, we would probably not show up and start critiquing every aspect of their culture, for better or worse. No, here's what we would do:

Whatever happens, conduct yourselves in a manner worthy of the gospel of Christ.

One thing is clear, we would not expect people who have no idea of the gospel to somehow miraculously conduct themselves in a manner worthy of the gospel. So if conducting ourselves in a manner worthy of the gospel cannot be reduced to believing and behaving, and ranting about those who don't, what does it mean?

What is conduct worthy of the gospel? Far from a thin veneer of moralistic behavior, the gospel is about becoming a new creation, a profoundly humble, pure-hearted, radically embracing person of extraordinary, holy love. It's not so much about what we don't do but who we are becoming together. It's about becoming a community of people whose relationships are telling a different story, who are writing an alternative ending to an otherwise broken storyline.

What if we thought of ourselves as those people, as citizens of another country who now find ourselves in a strange land? How would we want to conduct ourselves? Would we be mad at people who got abortions and went to casinos and smoked pot and regularly changed their gender identification? I suspect we might develop enormous compassion for them.

In the coming days, Paul will give us the most compelling vision on the planet of conduct worthy of the gospel. For now, he encourages us:

Stand firm in the one Spirit, striving together as one for the faith of the gospel.

The gospel is a team sport. Isn't it time we got off our high horses and joined that team in a new way (or maybe it's in an old way)?

The Prayer

Abba Father, we thank you for your Son, Jesus, who loves the broken and the confused and the ones who are lost and have no idea of it yet. Let us not forget we, too, were and sometimes are those people. We need a better vision of the gospel, not one of compromise but of love at another level. Come, Holy Spirit, shake us free from our complacent complaining. Get us in the game while there is still time. In Jesus' name we pray, amen.

The Questions

- Are you ready to put the kingdom of God ahead of the American dream—whatever that once was or would now become?
- Are you ready to claim your primary citizenship as a member of God's kingdom?
- Would this not be the absolute best thing for the country in which you live, no matter what country that is?

The Gospel in Two Grand Movements

12

PHILIPPIANS 1:29–30 | For it has been granted to you on behalf of Christ not only to believe in him, but also to suffer for him, since you are going through the same struggle you saw I had, and now hear that I still have.

Consider This

For it has been granted to you on behalf of Christ not only to believe in him, but also to suffer for him.

The gospel comes in two massive movements: believing and becoming. We believe in Jesus. We become like Jesus. Christ suffered on our behalf, and he grants to us the gift of suffering on his behalf. We must learn, though, what Jesus means by suffering. It is quite simple. Suffering, in the vision of the gospel, means love.

The first half of the gospel flows from John 3:16: "For God so loved the world that he gave his one and only Son, that whoever believes in him will not perish but have eternal life."

The second half of the gospel, perhaps serendipitously, issues from 1 John 3:16: "This is how we know what love is: Jesus Christ laid down his life for us. And we ought to lay down our lives for our brothers and sisters."

We see these two movements powerfully summarized in today's text: *For it has been granted to you on behalf of Christ not only to believe in him, but also to suffer for him.*

The path between believing and becoming is called the way of the cross. It brings us to another word beginning with the letter b: *belonging*. The way of the cross is the way of belonging to Jesus. To belong to Jesus means to become identified with him. It means ceasing to belong to the world and its pattern. To belong to Jesus is the pathway to becoming like him. "Christ in you" is the way Paul captures it (Col. 1:27). Suffering for him is nothing to be afraid of. The world has trained us to fear this word. Jesus will show us there is actually no better place on earth.

Buckle your Bible belts, my friends. This is where we are headed. For now, let this be your walking-around, breath prayer: "Jesus, I belong to you."

I want us to say it over and over and over until we find ourselves praying it.

Jesus, I belong to you. Jesus, I belong to you. Jesus, I belong to you. Jesus, I belong to you. Jesus, I belong to you. Jesus, I belong to you. Jesus, I belong to you. Jesus, I belong to you. Jesus, I belong to you. Jesus, I belong to you. Jesus, I belong to you.

Say a word of it with each step.

Believing and becoming. The way is belonging.

The Prayer

Abba Father, we thank you for your Son, Jesus, through whom you have determined to belong to us . . . to me. Grant us the gift of giving our lives to him. We want to belong to Jesus. We know it will mean no longer belonging to ourselves. This scares us, but, honestly, it scares us more to not go this way. Come, Holy Spirit, and grace us to walk in this way anew. We pray in Jesus' name, amen.

The Questions

- What do you make of this framework of the two halves of the gospel: believing and becoming?
- Why does the word *suffering* strike terror in us? Could it be because we belong to ourselves too much?
- Are you ready to enter a new chapter of belonging to Jesus? Will you begin with the simple breathing and walking prayer today? Will you make it a holy obsession?

Why Community Pantries Will Never Get It Done

13

PHILIPPIANS 2:1–2 | Therefore if you have any encouragement from being united with Christ, if any comfort from his love, if any common sharing in the Spirit, if any tenderness and compassion, then make my joy complete by being like-minded, having the same love, being one in spirit and of one mind.

Consider This

We have somehow come to equate our Christian witness to the world with the amount of good work we can do in the world. It does make sense, and it's not wrong. It's just not exactly right either. I mean, what distinguishes the service of Christians in the world from, say, the United Way or the Mormon Church? Is it just that we attach the name of Jesus to our service, as though that were a value added? Could it be our T-shirts?

Jesus seemed to articulate a different strategy when it came to the way his followers would be recognized and known in the world: "A new command I give you: Love one another. As I have loved you, so you must love one another. By this everyone will know that you are my disciples, if you love one another" (John 13:34–35).

Jesus is not advocating for a different kind of service provider in the world. He's building a different kind of community in the world. It is a community founded in the fellowship of the Holy Spirit, a group of people who are mysteriously caught up in and illumined by the interrelationships of the Father, Son, and Holy Spirit.

The reputation of the church in the world will never rise above the quality of the relationships within it. In fact, that is the church. After all, why did Jesus pray "that all of them may be one, Father, just as you are in me and I am in you. May they also be in us" (John 17:21a)?

Answer: "so that the world may believe that you have sent me" (v. 21b).

It makes sense, then, that Paul would put all his eggs in this basket.

Therefore if you have any encouragement from being united with Christ, if any comfort from his love, if any common sharing in the Spirit, if any tenderness and compassion, then make my joy complete by being like-minded, having the same love, being one in spirit and of one mind.

Paul gets it—where there is great love, miracles always happen. Consider this practical example. Why do we put so much stock in community pantries to help the poor? A poor person comes to our upper-middle-class church for help, and we dutifully send them down to the community pantry. What if we brought them into our community and loved them out of poverty—helped them get jobs, equipped them with the biblical wisdom to build a household economy, raised our children together, and so on? What if the community of the church, which is the fellowship of the Holy Spirit, was a place where the love for one another was so palpable nothing was impossible for them? Think of the witness this would be to the watching world!

Before I get angry e-mails, let me be clear. Community pantries are fine; they certainly help poor people. It's just they will never solve poverty. Only a community of ordinary relationships building itself up with extraordinary love will ever hope to do that.

And yes, these places do exist.*

---

* See Good Works, Inc., www.good-works.net, last accessed February 2020.

In the end, it doesn't have to do with poverty. It's about creating communities of true abundance.

The Prayer

Abba Father, we thank you for your Son, Jesus, who makes it all so clear to us. This is about loving one another. Forgive us for missing the point time and time again. Bring us into the mind of Christ in a new and living way. We belong to you, Jesus. In your name, we pray, amen.

The Questions

- Is this Pollyanna, pie-in-the-sky idealism I am articulating here? But is this not what the Bible is saying?
- Why do we put our stock in community pantries instead of embracing the poor in our local church communities?
- Why aren't we focusing on our relationships in the church at the microlevel?

14 Why Pride Is Not the Opposite of Humility— and What Is

PHILIPPIANS 2:3–4 ESV | Do nothing from selfish ambition or conceit, but in humility count others more significant than yourselves. Let each of you look not only to his own interests, but also to the interests of others.

Consider This

In Mark Twain's short story "The Esquimaux Maiden's Romance," Lasca, the maiden, quipped, "There's a breed of humility which is itself a species of showing off."*

Humility is tricky. As sure as you consider yourself a humble person, you can be sure you are not. What is humility? It often gets defined in ways that defy its very character. Most definitions come at humility in reference to oneself—something like self-abnegation.

Sometimes to get at a word's meaning it helps to consider its opposite. What do you think is the opposite of humility? The knee-jerk reaction answer: pride. I used to think of humility as thinking less of oneself. Later I thought of it as thinking of oneself less.

This is not how the Bible gets at humility. Today's text transports us into a whole new approach to how we think about humility. Check it out:

Do nothing from selfish ambition or conceit, but in humility count others more significant than yourselves. Let each of you look not only to his own interests, but also to the interests of others.

According to Scripture, the opposite of humility is not pride but selfishness. And therein lies the problem with our definitions. They are all self-referential. We can't even talk about humility without somehow referencing the self.

---

* Mark Twain, "The Esquimaux Maiden's Romance," See https://americanliterature .com/author/mark-twain/short-story/the-esquimaux-maidens-romance, last accessed February 2020.

Here's what I'm slowly learning. Humility is not about self at all. Humility is all about others. Humility is not putting yourself down; that's false humility. Humility is about lifting others up.

If I am about me, I am selfish. If I am about you, I am humble. I really do think it's that simple. However, there is a broken way of being all about others that is actually very selfish. It's called codependency. That's where most of us get stuck.

The journey of becoming a whole person is the pathway of being set free from the prison of self and liberated into the God-given capacity to love others. It's the way of the cross, the journey from being a "me" person to becoming a "you" person.

This is the mind of Christ.

The Prayer

Abba Father, we thank you for your Son, Jesus, the humble one. Set us free from the prison of our own selfishness that we might learn the way of holy love for others. Only you can do this, Jesus. We pray in your name, amen.

The Questions
- How do you define humility?
- Do you see how false humility works?
- What will it take for you to become truly humble? What is a step in that direction?

When Jesus Gives Us a Piece of His Mind

15

PHILIPPIANS 2:5 | In your relationships with one another, have the same mindset as Christ Jesus.

Consider This

Imagine having the same mindset as Jesus—learning to see like he sees, listen like he listens, think like he thinks, imagine like he imagines, and do things like he does things.

This, Paul says, is the secret to life. It's not as simple, though, as WWJD (What would Jesus do?), as though that were a simple thing in itself. The better question is HDJDI (How did Jesus do it?). Everything Jesus did, he did by the power of the indwelling person of the Holy Spirit. He was conceived by the Holy Spirit, baptized by the Holy Spirit, anointed by the Holy Spirit, gifted by the Holy Spirit, inspired by the Holy Spirit, empowered by the Holy Spirit, and infused with the Holy Spirit. He walked in the power of the Spirit, prayed in the language of the Spirit, healed in the power of the Spirit, loved in the way of the Spirit, and so on.

To "have the same mindset as Christ Jesus" means to be filled by the same power that filled Jesus—who is the person of the Holy Spirit.

How does this work? How does one acquire the mind of Christ Jesus? If Paul is calling us to have this mindset of

Jesus Christ, then we must be possessed of another mindset. Consider this instruction in Paul's letter to the Romans: "Do not conform to the pattern of this world, but be transformed by the renewing of your mind. Then you will be able to test and approve what God's will is—his good, pleasing and perfect will" (Rom. 12:2).

The pattern of this world is the mind of Adam. The pattern for our lives is the mind of Christ. Transformation happens as we willfully decide to turn away from the ingrained pattern of the broken and distorted mind of Adam (into which we are born) and place ourselves before God in a way that we can be transformed by the renewing of our mind.

How do we place ourselves before God? Let's back up one verse: "Therefore, I urge you, brothers and sisters, in view of God's mercy, to offer your bodies as a living sacrifice, holy and pleasing to God—this is your true and proper worship" (Rom. 12:1).

Sound familiar? It begins with belonging to God. Remember this: "Jesus, I belong to you." Are you staying with it? Jesus, I belong to you. Jesus, I belong to you. Say it until you mean it, and when you mean it, you will start to pray it.

Note something else here. Paul doesn't say offer your body. It's "bodies"—plural. And it's "a living sacrifice"—singular. And back to our text of the day, did you catch the opener that we are to have the mindset of Christ "in your relationships with one another"?

This is a team sport; it is not a solo flight. We are not transformed alone. I'm going to start pushing you harder and harder on this issue of banding together with a few other believers for the work of deep discipleship. The reason most of us are stuck is that we do not have the kinds of relationships it takes to sustain the level of work the Holy Spirit wills to do in our lives.

At Seedbed we have created an online platform whereby you can read the Daily Text as a small band/group and interact around it every day. Let me know when you are ready to give it a test drive. For now you can explore it at discipleshipbands.com.

The Prayer

Abba Father, we thank you for your Son, Jesus, who would bring us into his very mindset. Awaken us to the marvels of this truth and shake us from our satisfaction with thinking we've already got it. Come, Holy Spirit, and lead us in this way and into the kinds of relationships it will take to get there. We pray in Jesus' name, amen.

The Questions

- Do you see why WWJD will not work without HDJDI? Any experience with this?
- How do you think about the nature of the mindset of Christ? Are you actively pursuing this in a conscious fashion?
- Are you or have you ever been in a small enough group of people that you could really pursue deep discipleship together? What was that like? What has kept you from it?

16 | Down Is the New Up

PHILIPPIANS 2:6–7 ESV | [Christ Jesus,] who, though he was in the form of God, did not count equality with God a thing to be grasped, but emptied himself, by taking the form of a servant, being born in the likeness of men.

Consider This

We come now to one of the most visionary texts in all of the Bible. Philippians 2:6–11 comprise a fragment, perhaps the chorus, of one of the earliest hymns of the church. When the Philippians gathered for worship, this is what they sang.

When Romans 12:1 says, "Therefore, I urge you brothers and sisters, in view of God's mercy," this is the view Paul is referring to. In these few verses, the gospel is rehearsed with such profundity that it will be worthy of the rest of our lives to stand in awe.

As we enter in, it will serve us well to see the whole picture:

Have this mind among yourselves, which is yours in Christ Jesus, who, though he was in the form of God, did not count equality with God a thing to be grasped, but emptied himself, by taking the form of a servant, being born in the likeness of men. And being found in human form, he humbled himself by becoming obedient to the point of death, even death on a cross. Therefore God has highly exalted him and bestowed on him the name that is above every name, so that at the name of Jesus every knee should bow, in heaven and on earth and under the earth, and every tongue confess that Jesus Christ is Lord, to the glory of God the Father. (Phil. 2:5–11 ESV)

Note the massive V pattern formed by the text. Verses 6–8 take us from the very height of heights to the depth of depths. Verses 9–11 then take us back from the depths of death to glory in the highest. While the turning point is the death and resurrection of Jesus, the entire journey from top to bottom to top is the way of the cross. The cross cannot be reduced to a single day of Jesus' life. The cross is the whole tamale. The cross is the heart of God from before time. It's why the cross must become the shape of our lives.

Christian, this is your story. This is your song. This is your raison d'être. This is the way to "on earth as it is in heaven" (Matt. 6:10). This is the meaning of "But seek first the kingdom of God and his righteousness, and all these things will be added to you" (Matt. 6:33 ESV). This is the meaning of "Down Is the New Up."

From time to time I will lift up a text and commend it to us for what we in the Daily Text community call "rememberizing." Philippians 2:5–11 is one of those texts. Move it to the top of the order. There is simply no time to waste.

The Prayer

Abba Father, we thank you for your Son, Jesus, who is the way and the truth and the life, who calls us to follow him in this royal way of the holy cross. We confess we are afraid of this way. We trust you and yet we do not. Come, Holy Spirit, and fill us with insight that gives us courage that fires our faith to walk in this way. We pray in Jesus' name, amen.

The Questions

- On a scale of 1 to 10 (1 being lowest), how do you consider the mind of Christ to be the shaping dynamic of your life?
- Same scale: What is the level of your desire for the mind of Christ to be the shaping dynamic of your life?
- True or false: You are going to rememberize Philippians 2:5–11 as a life text.

17 | What to Do When Your Fullness Is Emptiness

PHILIPPIANS 2:7 | [R]ather, he made himself nothing
by taking the very nature of a servant,
being made in human likeness.

Consider This

Let's begin today by remembering the unfortunate mind of Adam. Adam and Eve were created in the image of God. They were human beings by nature. Jesus, a human being, was God by nature. It's interesting that Jesus, "being in very nature God, did not consider equality with God something to be used to his own advantage" (v. 6).

We can't say the same for Adam. Let's revisit the scene in Eden.

> "You will not certainly die," the serpent said to the woman. "For God knows that when you eat from it your eyes will be opened, and you will be like God, knowing good and evil."
>
> When the woman saw that the fruit of the tree was good for food and pleasing to the eye, and also desirable for gaining wisdom, she took some and ate it. She also gave some to her husband, who was with her, and he ate it. (Gen. 3:4–6)

Did you catch it? The serpent said, "You will be like God." Adam and Eve, the ones created in the very image of God, decided equality with God was something to be grasped. And grasp they did.

This fateful decision had the effect of creating just the opposite pattern. Remember, the mind of Christ forms the V pattern. The mind of Adam, in opposite fashion, forms the Λ pattern.

The ones who were servants of all of creation determined to be gods. The one who was God determined to be a servant. The image-bearers of God who had been given everything still needed to try to make themselves something. The Son of God made himself nothing.

The Greek term behind "made himself nothing" is kenosis. It means to empty oneself. Why did Jesus empty himself? He did it for love. The one who was full made himself empty so we who are empty could be made full.

In order for sinful people like us to be justified before a holy God, we must simply accept Jesus' work on our behalf. That is the first half of the gospel. The second half of the gospel, or sanctification, is the process of taking on the mind of Christ. This means emptying ourselves of all we thought would be fullness in order that we might be filled with all the fullness of God.

Because we are born into the mind of Adam we, too, make the fateful choice to grasp for equality with God. We do it by choosing to trust someone (including ourselves) or something other than God. We do this because of our own insecurity. We are not secure in and of ourselves. We were never meant to be. We need God.

Unfortunately, we will trust in just about anything and everything under the sun but God. The result is that we build false security, which becomes a false self. In an attempt to be secure, we fill ourselves up with everything but the one thing that will give us ultimate security—God. Growing in the grace of the gospel means a long process of emptying ourselves of all this falseness—this emptiness that masquerades as fullness—that we might be filled with true fullness. We think the way to life is up. It is down. It's why we say, "Down Is the New Up." Descent defines the way of the cross. Only in the fullness of God will we find the fullness of our true self.

Who doesn't want that?

It's why Jesus was so good to tell us, "For whoever wants to save their life will lose it, but whoever loses their life for me will save it" (Luke 9:24).

The Prayer

Abba Father, we thank you for your Son, Jesus, who is the fullness of God. Show us the upside-downness of our lives. Teach us that the way down is the way up. We are so tired of trying to fill ourselves up when only you can do that. Come, Holy Spirit, and lead us in this way of descent, following Jesus in the way of the cross. We pray in Jesus' name, amen.

The Questions

- Do you see the reversal happening between the mind of Adam and the mind of Christ?
- Have you or are you filling yourself with false security? Do you see the emptiness in that?
- Do you have a sense of your own false self—the shadow self you have constructed over the years attempting to make your life work apart from complete dependence on God? Are you ready to take the next step in deconstructing it?

Oh Lord, It's Hard to Be Humble

18

PHILIPPIANS 2:8 | And being found in appearance as a man, he humbled himself
by becoming obedient to death—
even death on a cross!

Consider This

Before going further, let's take a minute to review our learnings.

Remember, the way of the cross is the long, slow, glorious, and often arduous process of moving from Λ to V.

We are growing up by growing down. The way is descent. The measure of all the fullness of God is found at the cross.

The process leads to the transformation of our default mind, the mind of Adam (Λ), into the mind of Jesus Christ (V).

The only way to find this way is to follow Jesus. This is the way that leads to the truth, which becomes the life. And, sadly, few find it (Matt. 7:14). We are mostly stuck somewhere in between the gift of justification by grace through faith and the grace of sanctification by grace through faith.

The primary reason we are stuck is we do not have the kind of relationships it takes to foment and foster this kind of transformation. We call it "banded discipleship."

And being found in appearance as a man,
> *he humbled himself*
> *by becoming obedient to death—*
>> *even death on a cross!*

The one who was whole made himself broken so that we who are broken could be made whole.

He humbled himself. Humility, remember, is not defined in relation to oneself. Humility is not about self; it is about others. Jesus' humility was displayed in his obedience to his Father. Jesus did not put himself down; he lifted his Father up. He did not put sinners down; he lifted us up. He descended all the way down to the cross, even to the kingdom of hell, that he might lift the broken human race all the way up to the kingdom of heaven.

Our humility begins when we become obedient to God. As we learn to obey God from a posture of humble love, we will grow humble in our relationships with others.

Why "obedient to death"? The decision of human beings to disobey God effectively makes us obedient to death. Sin means obedience to death. Now, when the one who is without sin is obedient unto death, he destroys death. Death, in essence, is swallowed up by life.

Sin and death are not creative, but they are sophisticated. Consider how the children of Adam and Eve turned on one another out of jealousy. Cain, grasping for his own equality with God, murdered his brother Abel. This quest for dominance and control led through the days of Noah and to complete destruction. It led all the way to the proud tower of Babel. Remember why they built it:* "Then they said, 'Come, let us build ourselves a city, with a tower that reaches to the heavens, so that we may make a name for ourselves; otherwise we will be scattered over the face of the whole earth'" (Gen. 11:4).

This is the ultimate marker of ascent: "so that we may make a name for ourselves." Contrast this with the one who humbled himself:

And being found in appearance as a man,
   he humbled himself
   by becoming obedient to death—
     even death on a cross!

---

* See John Walton's video, "The Meaning of the Tower of Babel," https://www
.seedbed.com/tower-babel/.

The Prayer

Abba Father, we thank you for your Son, Jesus, who is the personification of humility. Teach us to walk in his way of obedience, an obedience born of love and trust. We want to be humble, Lord, yet we are filled with pride. Lead us to the cross where we might be emptied of this, for our sake and for your glory. We pray in Jesus' name, amen.

The Questions

- What do you think of this connection between obedience and humility? How do you see that they are related?
- How are you coming along in your understanding of humility as not being defined in reference to oneself but with respect to others?
- What stands in the way of you humbling yourself?

19 The Problem with Self-Actualization

PHILIPPIANS 2:9 | Therefore God exalted him to the highest place

and gave him the name that is above every name.

Consider This

"Then they said, 'Come, let us build ourselves a city, with a tower that reaches to the heavens, so that we may make a name for ourselves; otherwise we will be scattered over the face of the whole earth'" (Gen. 11:4).

They wanted to make a name for themselves. Did you catch the turn in today's text?

Therefore God exalted him to the highest place
and gave him the name that is above every name.

We spend so much of our lives striving to become somebody, to make a name for ourselves. All the while, God, our good Father, stands ready to give us a name. In fact, to become a Christian is to be given his name, the one that is above every name. We are baptized into his name. Even better, we are baptized in the name of the Father and the Son and the Holy Spirit.

At the very starting line of the Christian faith we receive everything we will ever need for the life we were created to live. We are blessed as the beloved sons and daughters of a Father who is well pleased with us. We are cleansed from the stain of sin, washed in the atoning blood of the Lamb, pardoned from sin's cruel penalty, and given the gift of eternal life. We are marked, sealed, and gifted by the Holy Spirit, empowered to live a life of holy love. All of this is present at baptism and must be claimed and confirmed over and over again.

We stand, so to speak, at the top of the V, prepared to descend into the valley of the cross, literally clothed in Christ. Now this patterned path must be walked again and again and again, as the Holy Spirit leads us in the way that progressively causes these truths to become enfleshed in our everyday lives.

The challenge is our bent toward climbing, grasping, and otherwise pursuing paths of our own making, for our own glory, to make a name for ourselves. One cannot ascend and descend at the same time. To choose descent, which is to follow Jesus, means all we once held dear as the substance of our identities (our false selves) must be dismantled and discarded.

If I am honest, I loathe equality with others. I want to be better, to have a better name, a better claim to fame, to be more important, sought after, and revered. When I came to the experienced discovery that I was the beloved son of an adoring Father (irrespective of any of my accomplishments and all of my failures), it became clear for me to embrace this gifted identity would mean laying aside every other claim that gave me distinction or disqualified me. Why? Because if this is true of me, then it is true of you too. If I am a beloved son and you are a beloved son/daughter, we can then be siblings without rivalry. We can love one another as we love ourselves.

This quest for distinction runs so deep in us. It often goes by the name of self-actualization, and, depending on how this term is understood, it can be helpful or a great hindrance. I prefer the language of baptismal-actualization or grace-actualization, or the realization of Christ-in-you. We must come to realize that only the unmerited favor and grace of God gives us a true sense of self, one we did nothing to disqualify ourselves from or deserve.

Every other way we attempt to scratch out a self-identity in this world is false, leaving us hopelessly bound in the slavery of keeping up appearances, holding it all together,

Maslow's hierarchy

and otherwise stuck in a self-absorbed existence (no matter how much it may look otherwise).

In short, the reality of the gift of grace in Jesus Christ unravels the slavish economy of our false self. The only way we will ever set our foot on the path of descent comes through the audacity of claiming this gifted identity, this blessed name for oneself. Everything else is just another trip up the mountain and a fall down the other side.

The Prayer

Abba Father, we thank you for your Son, Jesus, whose gifted name is above every name. Thank you for the cross by which he leads us into this gift of sharing in his name and nature. We confess we are filled with a self of our own making. We are ready to let it go, but we need so much help to do so. Come, Holy Spirit, and apply these verities in our innermost beings. We pray in Jesus' name, amen.

The Questions

- How would you begin to describe your false self, the identity you have constructed apart from the grace of God (one that either distinguishes you or disqualifies you)?
- What do you make of this contrast between self-actualization and baptismal-actualization or the realization of Christ-in-you?
- Do you compare yourself with others? Why do you do this other than a need to find yourself somehow distinguished from them (for better or worse)? What does this say about your sense of self and identity?

20 Is "Jesus Christ Is Lord" True in Your Life?

PHILIPPIANS 2:10–11 ESV | [S]o that at the name of Jesus every knee should bow, in heaven and on earth and under the earth, and every tongue confess that Jesus Christ is Lord, to the glory of God the Father.

Consider This

We come to the end of the song in today's text. We began at the top left point of the V at the throne of God. We end at the top right point of the V, again at the throne of God. We behold the glory of it all at the very bottom, at the foot of the cross.

The mind of Adam is precisely the opposite. We begin at the bottom left of the Λ pattern. Though given everything, even the image of God, we determined to grasp for ascent to equality with God. We reached the top with a great tower designed to make a great name for ourselves. The result of all our grasping was a great falling down the other side. The Λ forms a dead-end cycle of determination, disappointment, and despair. The V, quite the opposite, begins with discontent, leading to a descent into our broken ways where we reach the bottom and find surrender and dependence on God. The way back up is one of being lifted into delight in God and onward to true devotion to others.

Remember what happened at our Babylonian building project: "That is why it was called Babel—because there the

Lord confused the language of the whole world. From there the Lord scattered them over the face of the whole earth" (Gen. 11:9).

See what happened in today's text. The great gathering has already begun at the cross, eyes lifted to the throne of God, every nation, tribe, and tongue making the declaration, "Jesus Christ is Lord"! We do not return to speaking the same language, but we do learn to say the same thing.

Jesus Christ is Lord. This is not software-agreement language. This is the totalizing, all-consuming truth of the universe. That's not enough. Lest this truth, "Jesus Christ is Lord," become our personal, everyday, walking-around lifestyle, it means nothing. These are not mere words, but a manifesto. These words must be parsed, translated, conjugated, and implemented to the most granular detail of our lives. Jesus Christ is Lord!

To the extent that I continue to run the pattern of the world (∧), climbing my own mountain for my own glory (no matter how much it may benefit others), I am a living denial of the lordship of Jesus Christ. As I follow Jesus downward into the valley of the cross, the valley of vision, he will lift me back up the other side, and, for the joy of the cross, I will run in the way of the V again and again and again.

The Prayer

Abba Father, we thank you for your Son, Jesus, whose name is above every name. We want to follow him, yet we cling so tightly to ourselves. Come, Holy Spirit, and give us grace to let go of ourselves that we might follow Jesus with our whole hearts.

We are weary of our own determination to make something of ourselves. We are ready to surrender all to you so that we might become who you made us to be. We pray in Jesus' name, amen.

The Questions

- How do you relate to these contrasting patterns of the Λ and the V? Does this resonate?
- Is your discontent with the status quo of your life at a place where you are ready to put your feet on the path of descent?
- Where are you challenged in your everyday life to live out the confession "Jesus Christ is Lord"?

21 If Sin Has Lost Its Power, Why Is It So Powerful?

PHILIPPIANS 2:12–13 | Therefore, my dear friends, as you have always obeyed—not only in my presence, but now much more in my absence—continue to work out your salvation with fear and trembling, for it is God who works in you to will and to act in order to fulfill his good purpose.

Consider This

On the point of salvation, the Bible offers two truths that seem contradictory at first glance yet turn out to be profoundly complementary.

Truth #1: We cannot work for our salvation.
Truth #2: We must work out our salvation.

Salvation is by grace, which means there is nothing we can do to earn it. It is the free gift of God. Like any gift, it must be freely received. In this case, it must be received by faith. This means we must learn to act as if we have received it.

Salvation is also a responsibility—as in the God-given ability to respond to grace. God works grace into our lives. We must work it out through our lives.

Now, here's the kicker: though we are sinners, God gives us the power to not sin. We don't believe this. We base our understanding not on the truth of God's Word but on our own broken experience.

We are all acting in faith in one way or another. If we are not acting on the faith that sin has lost its power and that we have the power to defeat sin in our lives, it necessarily follows that our faith is not in the power of God but in the power of sin. We perhaps believe Jesus has saved us from the penalty of sin, but we effectively believe that sin still has power. It's a hard truth to reckon with when we put it this way—which is why we don't tend to put it this way.

The faith of a Christian is the sure confidence that God has done something so profoundly revolutionary in our innermost being that everything about us is being made new. Sin has not gone anywhere; it has simply lost its power. We are to:

Continue to work out [our] salvation with fear and trembling.

Maybe what we are missing is the fear and trembling part. Perhaps the bumper sticker caption for our time is this: "I'm not perfect, just forgiven." There's certainly no "fear and trembling" in that. It's casual Christianity or easy beliefs. I think the bumper sticker caption for the New Testament is quite the opposite: "I'm not just forgiven; I'm being made perfect." Now that's awe-inspiring. To be clear, this word, *perfect*, does not mean flawless or without error. It means full, as in the fullness of Jesus Christ, which is the fullness of holy love.

It's the fear and trembling that are missing. And why fear and trembling?

It is God who works in you to will and to act in order to fulfill his good purpose.

The fact of God working in us to accomplish his will is awe-inspiring. It's hard to fathom. A holy and righteous and all-powerful God at work in frail, fragile, sinful human beings? Holy sanctification, Batman!

I'm almost sure I don't take this seriously enough—the God of the universe working in my everyday, walking-around, Krispy Kreme–donut-eating life?

To work out my salvation in fear and trembling doesn't mean to cower in timidity. It means to become increasingly attuned to the living, active presence of *God in my body*, forming and forging the mind of Christ, filling me with the fullness of the Holy Spirit.

Stay with that thought. More on that tomorrow.

The Prayer

Abba Father, we thank you for your Son, Jesus, who has defeated sin and death. We want to stop living like sin still has power. We need your Spirit to awaken us to a new way of understanding and living. Show us what it means to work this out in our everyday lives. We pray in Jesus' name, amen.

The Questions

- So how about it? Do you believe sin has lost its power or do you believe sin still has its power?
- Are you ready to break free from the arrested development of living like sin is still in power?
- Will you spend the next five minutes meditating over these words: "Jesus, you are alive in me"?

This Is Not an AA Advertisement

22

PHILIPPIANS 2:14–16 ESV | Do all things without grumbling or disputing, that you may be blameless and innocent, children of God without blemish in the midst of a crooked and twisted generation, among whom you shine as lights in the world, holding fast to the word of life, so that in the day of Christ I may be proud that I did not run in vain or labor in vain.

Consider This

Why do people go to Alcoholics Anonymous (AA)?

Because they are struggling with alcohol? Obviously. There's a better answer. People go to Alcoholics Anonymous because it works. AA meetings end with the group joining hands and saying to one another, "Keep coming back. It works if you work it."

AA works because people there are working out their salvation with fear and trembling, because they know God is working in them to bring about his purposes in their lives.

Recovering the same mind in us that was in Christ Jesus requires something akin to AA to bring it about. Did you notice the term I used there—*recovering*? AA is about recovery. So is the Christian faith. The Christian life is about recovering the image of God in our everyday lives. This process takes the Word of God, the Spirit of God, and the people of God. It will not happen in isolation as a fruit of our cloistered quiet times.

What we need is Sinners Anonymous. Hang on! Isn't that what church is supposed to be? If I were in charge of church across the whole country, here's what I would do. I would cancel our regularly scheduled programs and require everyone go visit an AA meeting that week instead. Why? Because I want the followers of Jesus to witness what happens when people show up in a room together and get honest and real with one another.

These people start to shine like stars in the sky in the midst of a crooked and warped generation. People go to AA and they keep going for one reason. There is an ever-growing group of people who are growing in freedom, staying sober, and otherwise living lives that work. It is compelling and even irresistible.

I meet every Monday morning with two other men in a kind of Sinners Anonymous group. We call it a discipleship band. Throughout the week we read together. Once a week we meet together. We live in different states so we link up on a call. We spend a little over an hour together asking one another five questions. While together and throughout the whole process, we pray together. We are working out our salvation in fear and trembling because we are coming to learn together that God is working in us to bring about his purposes in our lives. Banding together is the most inglorious glorious work I do all week.

My holy ambition is to get you banded together into a discipleship band. It's not enough to write about all this. It's not enough to read it. I consider you my parish, and, as your pastor, I'm not going to rest until we are all working out our salvation together and getting on with the gospel's glorious work in our lives and worlds.

Then I will say with Paul:

so that in the day of Christ I may be proud that I did not run in vain or labor in vain.

The Prayer

Abba Father, we thank you for your Son, Jesus, whose first act of ministry was to band together with twelve other people. We want to be about the real work of the gospel in our lives and in the world. We have wasted so much time on so much religious activity that hasn't gone anywhere. Lead us to real people to work through the real stuff. We pray in Jesus' name, amen.

The Questions

- Have you ever been to an AA meeting or other kind of recovery group? What was that like?
- If you are not working out your salvation in fear and trembling in community with a few other people, how are you doing it? How is that going?
- ✳ Are you ready to go to the next level, knowing that level will be downward? What is holding you back?

23 How Dangerous Are Your Prayers?

PHILIPPIANS 2:17–18 ESV | Even if I am to be poured out as a drink offering upon the sacrificial offering of your faith, I am glad and rejoice with you all. Likewise you also should be glad and rejoice with me.

Consider This

In biblical terms, a drink offering means basically to pour out a cup of wine as an act of worship to God. The worshipper does not drink any of it themselves. It is all poured out as a sign of the victory and the joy of God. In other words, it is a complete sacrifice.

In this letter to the Philippians, Paul is casting a bold vision for us to make a totalizing offer of our lives to Jesus. When Paul calls for us to have the same mind in us that was in

Christ Jesus (v. 5), this is what he means. The best part is, Paul not only calls us to this life, he lives it out before our very eyes.

How do we do this? It begins with praying dangerous prayers and the willingness to have the Holy Spirit bend our lives in the shape of those prayers. The best people to learn this from are people whose lives have proved it true. What dangerous prayers did they pray? One such person and prayer comes to mind in John Wesley. I want to share an excerpt of a dangerous prayer from his life. It is from his covenant service, which many traditionally pray on New Year's Eve or Day. I commend it to us as an everyday prayer.

> I am no longer my own, but thine. Put me to what thou wilt, rank me with whom thou wilt. Put me to doing, put me to suffering. Let me be employed for thee or laid aside for thee, exalted for thee or brought low for thee. Let me be full, let me be empty. Let me have all things, let me have nothing. I freely and heartily yield all things to thy pleasure and disposal. And now, O glorious and blessed God, Father, Son and Holy Spirit, thou art mine, and I am thine. So be it. And the covenant which I have made on earth, let it be ratified in heaven. Amen.*

---

* See the Seedbed seedling, "Watchnight: John Wesley's Covenant Renewal Service."

The Prayer

Abba Father, we thank you for your Son, Jesus, whose life was and continues to be the ultimate drink offering. Come, Holy Spirit, and give us the fullness of him that our lives might be poured out for his glory. It is in his name we pray, amen.

The Questions

- Does this sound completely unreasonable to you—that your life would be poured out as a drink offering?
- What are you afraid of when it comes to making an unconditional offering of your life to God?
- What are you afraid of when it comes to not making an unconditional offering of your life to God? Which fear is greater?

24 When Everything in Your Life Is Hard

PHILIPPIANS 2:19–21 | I hope in the Lord Jesus to send Timothy to you soon, that I also may be cheered when I receive news about you. I have no one else like him, who will show genuine concern for your welfare. For everyone looks out for their own interests, not those of Jesus Christ.

Consider This

Don't you love it how Paul just breaks out of the most massive Christological hymn in the history of hymns (a.k.a.

Philippians 2:6–11) and now he's onto his to-do list as relates to the Philippians? He's sending emissaries and making travel plans.

Not only is Paul's life a living crucible of the gospel he is preaching, he has a protégé in whom the gospel is also flourishing: Timothy.

Note Paul's metric for what gospel flourishing looks like:

I have no one else like him, who will show genuine concern for your welfare.

It's got me asking myself, *Do I show genuine concern for the welfare of other people? Or am I primarily concerned about my own welfare?* Honestly, I don't think I land in either of those places. I am somewhere in the mushy middle. The next verse instructs me in a fresh way:

For everyone looks out for their own interests, not those of Jesus Christ.

I'm not sure I am making this connection between showing genuine concern for the welfare of others and the interests of Jesus Christ. Let me state that more emphatically. The interest of Jesus Christ is served by my showing genuine concern for the welfare of others and not looking out for my own interests.

I'll be honest with you. I am living in a season of time right now where everything about my life is hard. My own interests feel overwhelming a lot of the time. In fact, I am living in a season where I don't have the bandwidth for too much genuine concern for the welfare of others. In other words, it's not in my self-interest to show genuine concern for the welfare of others. It's not that I don't care. It's that I don't have the capacity. I believe the Lord allows times like these in our lives to grow us beyond our self-interest and to build into us new Holy Spirit–inspired capacities. I believe times like these, which I know many of you are also facing, are those times when the Holy Spirit whispers, "My grace is sufficient for you, for my power is made perfect in weakness" (2 Cor. 12:9).

That doesn't make it any easier, just a lot more hopeful. I'm beginning to see my own job description in a lot simpler terms. It goes like this: look out for the interests of Jesus Christ by showing genuine concern for the welfare of others. Period. There is a word that captures this whole thing: *love*.

The Prayer

Abba Father, we thank you for your Son, Jesus, who has shown us what genuine concern for the welfare of others looks like. It's extraordinary. We don't have this capacity, Lord, but we know you do, and if you are in us, then your capacity can be ours. Thank you for leading us in this way. We pray in Jesus' name, amen.

The Questions

- Can you remember a time in your life where everything was hard? What did you learn in those days?
- Could Paul count on you to "show genuine concern" for the welfare of others?
- Why do most people look out for their own interests and not for the interests of Jesus Christ?

Henry - sun poisoning

The Gospel of Multilevel Marketing

25

PHILIPPIANS 2:22–24 | But you know that Timothy has proved himself, because as a son with his father he has served with me in the work of the gospel. I hope, therefore, to send him as soon as I see how things go with me. And I am confident in the Lord that I myself will come soon.

Consider This

Do you have a downline? Do you know what a downline is? It's a multilevel marketing concept. Your downline is the people you have recruited to sell whatever it is you are selling and the people they have recruited to sell whatever it is you are selling—all of whose sales accrue to your benefit.

Now, take away the cringeworthy elements of multilevel marketing and apply the downline concept to the gospel. Paul has an extraordinary downline, and disciple 1-A in that downline is Timothy.

But you know that Timothy has proved himself, because as a son with his father he has served with me in the work of the gospel.

In Paul's second letter to Timothy, he instructs Timothy concerning his own downline, which, remember, is also part of Paul's downline: "You have heard me teach things that have been confirmed by many reliable witnesses. Now teach these truths to other trustworthy people who will be able to pass them on to others" (2 Tim. 2:2 NLT).

So here's the questions: Do you have a downline? Have you ever thought about whose downline you belong to? Can you think of a person who would claim to be in your downline? I didn't grow up in a church context where this concept was lifted up as a real value. There was value placed on being a good, God-fearing Christian citizen who helped other people. There was a lot of lip service paid to the idea of "making disciples," but the notion of being a disciple-maker was just not there.

So many churches have some version of "making disciples for Jesus Christ" in their official mission statement. What we really need to be doing is making disciple-makers. See the difference? If our goal was to get chocolate chip cookies to every person in the world, what would be better—to make as many chocolate chip cookies as we could make or to make as many chocolate chip cookie–makers as we could make? Though seemingly similar, they are quite different missions.

Jesus made it clear. Our commission is to make disciples. The church organization is never going to get that done. Until we start making disciple-makers, we are just making cookies.

The Prayer

Abba Father, we thank you for your Son, Jesus, who is the ultimate disciple-maker. Bring us into the disciple-maker tradition of Jesus. Come, Holy Spirit, and make us disciple-makers. We pray in Jesus' name, amen.

The Questions

- So what's the shape of your downline?
- What keeps you from being a disciple-maker?
- How do you see the difference between a broad commitment to making disciples and the distinctive responsibility and work of being a disciple-maker?

Are You a Real Gospel Soldier?

26

PHILIPPIANS 2:25–28 | But I think it is necessary to send back to you Epaphroditus, my brother, co-worker and fellow soldier, who is also your messenger, whom you sent to take care of my needs. For he longs for all of you and is distressed because you heard he was ill. Indeed he was ill, and almost died. But God had mercy on him, and not on him only but also on me, to spare me sorrow upon sorrow. Therefore I am all the more eager to send him, so that when you see him again you may be glad and I may have less anxiety.

Consider This

In the ancient world, the state didn't take care of prisoners. This is why the Philippian church sent Epaphroditus. Don't you love it how the Philippians owned Paul's welfare? Of all the churches, they stepped up big time. That's why Paul is so grateful to them. Epaphroditus likely contracted some kind of illness on his way to Rome, but rather than turn back, he risked his life to fulfill the mission. When he arrived and began to assist Paul, his sickness got worse, taking him to the brink of death.

Everybody has trouble in life, but when you raise the stakes on your involvement in the work of the gospel of Jesus Christ, you can expect more trouble.

It's very interesting, the ways Paul refers to Epaphroditus in today's text. Did you catch it: "my brother, co-worker and fellow soldier"? There's a progression here. Epaphroditus, by virtue of following Jesus, is Paul's "brother." By virtue of coming alongside Paul in Rome, he became a "co-worker" in the gospel. Paul takes it a giant step further when he calls him a "fellow soldier." We need to catch the weight of this. Paul doesn't just throw this around as in, "Onward, Christian soldier." He means Epaphroditus stepped out of the comforts of Philippi's suburban life and onto the frontlines of the war and took on enemy fire. Epaphroditus's illness was an act of spiritual warfare. Satan tried to take him out.

Sometimes we overinterpret the bad things that happen to us as spiritual warfare. When we claim spiritual warfare, we, in effect, claim our status as soldiers. We must ask ourselves: Why would Satan bother with attacking me? How is my life and work threatening his kingdom? The term *spiritual warfare* has come to be used quite casually.

By way of an opposite analogy, consider the war on terrorism. If you are related to suspected terrorists or harbor suspected terrorists or in any way help them or fund them or get involved with them on social media or anywhere else, you can bet that someone in law enforcement is going to be assigned to watch you like a hawk. By your active involvement, you make yourself an enemy of the state, who will do everything they can to name you an enemy combatant, which empowers them to come after you with everything they've got.

Satan is real. Principalities and powers and rulers and authorities are real. There is a real kingdom of darkness (Eph. 6:12). The minute you step out of the ranks of casual Christianity and offer yourself for an assignment in God's kingdom, you enter the ranks of enemy combatants, and you can bet some demonic agent of darkness is being assigned to you.

This is why Paul, in his letter to the Ephesians, gets so explicit about putting on the full armor of God (Eph. 6:11, 13–17). Domesticated casual Christianity is no threat to the enemy. I've been writing a lot of personal letters lately to people who have given of their resources to our work with Seedbed. Be assured if you did this, your name is on my prayer list, but it is also on another list. You are making yourself an enemy combatant to the kingdom of darkness. Put on the full armor of God.

I don't want to overestimate my role and work in the kingdom of God, but I now find myself behind enemy lines and deep in hostile territory. For the past seven years, I have been under withering enemy fire. I know I am to the apostle Paul as a foot soldier is to General Patton, but the battle is real. I consider all of you as brothers and sisters in the Lord, many of you as co-laborers in the gospel, and still others as fellow soldiers in the thick of this war on darkness. Some of you have jumped into the foxhole with me. I am eternally grateful, but in case I was not clear: now is the time to put on your armor.

The Prayer

Abba Father, we thank you for your Son, Jesus, who will win the battle. Thank you that though we take on fire and may get sick to the point of death and even die, we are invincible in him. We want to be more in the line of fire for your kingdom. We don't want to reach the end and realize we played it safe. We pray in Jesus' name, amen.

The Questions

- Have you ever been under real spiritual attack and warfare? Have you overinterpreted spiritual warfare before? Underinterpreted it?
- Are you willing to offer yourself to Jesus for an assignment in his kingdom (not to become a professional Christian but to get in the fight)?
- Anybody out there want to enlist?

27 Are You Raising Your Hand Yet?

PHILIPPIANS 2:29–30 | So then, welcome him in the Lord with great joy, and honor people like him, because he almost died for the work of Christ. He risked his life to make up for the help you yourselves could not give me.

Consider This

Epaphroditus raised his hand. He took on a hard assignment. We still tell his war story today. We honor Epaphroditus and people like him. From the first century to the twenty-first century, Jesus establishes his kingdom, on earth as it is in heaven, through the faith, courage, and obedience of ordinary people like Epaphroditus.

Let's remember how Paul got to Philippi in the first place. Remember his dream where the man from Macedonia beckoned him to come to them? Philippi was the first destination. Here's the account from Acts 16:

> On the Sabbath we went outside the city gate to the river, where we expected to find a place of prayer. We sat down and began to speak to the women who had gathered there. One of those listening was a woman from the city of Thyatira named Lydia, a dealer in purple cloth. She was a worshiper of God. The Lord opened her heart to respond to Paul's message. When she and the members of her household were baptized, she invited us to her home. "If you consider me a believer in the Lord," she said, "come and stay at my house." And she persuaded us. (vv. 13–16)

Paul saw a man in his dream, but it was a woman who would bring it to fulfillment. Lydia raised her hand, became the first Christian in all of Europe, and quickly followed as the leader of the first church-planting team.

No one knows the story at the outset. They just raise their hand and do the next right thing. It's never about the numbers—only the name. They think big, act small, pray hard, and love well. O Lord, I want to be in that number— found in that name!

My mind runs to eighteenth-century England and colonial America. John Wesley was looking for someone to go to America to encourage the fledgling Methodists in the new world. Twenty-six-year-old Frank Asbury raised his hand. He took on a hard assignment. He arrived to find 316 Methodist society members. He rode an average of 6,000 miles a year on horseback, a total of some 270,000 miles. He preached upward of 15,000 sermons, ordained four thousand clergymen, and presided over 224 annual conferences of the burgeoning movement. He made an annual salary of eighty dollars. Forty-five years later, the movement had grown to 215,000.[*]

To this day, those Methodists were the first and only group in history to plant a church in every county in this country. I keep thinking to myself, *Why not now, Lord? Why not us?*

I see that hand.

The Prayer

Abba Father, we thank you for your Son, Jesus, who, being in very nature God did not consider equality with God something to be grasped, but he raised his hand. Thank you for Paul and Timothy and Epaphroditus and Lydia and John and Frank and Jessica and Scot and Julian and Mary and Sid and Micah and David and Mark and Andrew and Andy and Jessie

---

[*] See the Seedbed seedling, "The Dedicatory Address of Calvin Coolidge at the Unveiling of the Equestrian Statue of Francis Asbury."

and Holly and Darlene and so many more who have raised their hand. Come, Holy Spirit, and increase this tribe. O Lord, we want to be in that number—found in that name—the name in which we pray, Jesus, amen.

The Questions

- How are you inspired by the Holy Spirit today?
- Is your hand raised?
- What holds you back?

Why "If You're Happy and You Know It" Is the Wrong Song | 28

PHILIPPIANS 3:1–4A ESV | Finally, my brothers [and sisters], rejoice in the Lord. To write the same things to you is no trouble to me and is safe for you.

Look out for dogs, look out for evildoers, look out for those who mutilate the flesh. For we are the circumcision, who worship by the Spirit of God and glory in Christ Jesus and put no confidence in the flesh—though I myself have reason for confidence in the flesh also.

Consider This

These letters of Paul instruct us on so many levels. There's a word in the opening verse of today's text we have seen no less than five times already. Did you catch it? The word is rejoice. An untutored reader might surmise that Paul was on the top of the world.

Paul was anywhere but on the top of the world. He was living in the pit of hell, a Roman prison cell. And he is rejoicing all over the place. Before it's all said and done, Paul will mention "joy" or "rejoice" some sixteen times. We learn something very important about joy here. Joy is not happiness. It's not a feeling or an emotion. Joy is not positive thinking. Joy is a fruit of the Holy Spirit (Gal. 5:22–23). Joy is supernatural. It is a wellness that transcends health, a state of being that eclipses emotion, and an inner realism that overwhelms apparent reality. Though it transcends the ephemeral notion of earthly emotion, we might think of joy as the primary emotion of the realm of eternal reality. Joy is that deep inner conviction that though things are not right, everything is going to be alright.

Joy is not an emotion because joy is not something that happens to us like a feeling. Joy is not happiness. Joy most typically originates from a place of suffering and sadness. Joy is an action. It's why Paul rejoices. Joy is experienced by those who exercise their faith through rejoicing.

One of the great gifts of the African American church to the body of Christ is their long-standing tradition of joy. As a race, they know suffering and sadness all too well, yet they will not be defined by it. While my church was teaching us, "If you're happy and you know it, clap your hands," across town they were singing, "His eye is on the sparrow." The African American church teaches us how to rejoice.

I will never forget being in a particular worship service a few years back on a Sunday morning in a pretty much all-white church. Near the end of the service, the pastor noticed the well-known African American vocalist BeBe Winans was in attendance and invited him to bring greetings and close the service in song. We all expected (and were looking forward to) him singing one of his Grammy award–winning, multiple-platinum-selling songs. He began to tell us of the really hard things he had faced in his life in recent years and how he had been in the lowest of low places. Then he started talking about Jesus, and, after a few minutes, he began rejoicing, and then he broke into a song. It was a song none of us had ever heard before. It had only four words: "Everything's gonna be alright."

As he sang them over and over, the Spirit ushered the whole place into singing them with him. This white church began to shed its whiteness as the hospitality of the African American gospel tradition embraced us. That morning there were people with cancer, and people grieving losses, and people on the brink of ruin and in the depths of despair, and people in troubled marriages, and families with wayward children—and every last one of them was rejoicing, knowing that though they may lose the battle, Jesus had won the war. Everything's gonna be alright.

I bet we sang that song for no less than twenty minutes, and we could have gone on for twenty more. No one cared. Somehow we knew in a way we hadn't known before that, though weeping may endure for the night, joy would come with the morning (Psalm 30:5). We were literally being carried away on the wings rejoicing. I will never forget it. Joy invaded us as the Spirit lifted us. It wasn't clappy happy. It wasn't euphoric escapism. It was heaven come down—eternal life breaking in. I can still hear the tune, and, to this day, I find myself singing it just under my breath all the time. Thank you, BeBe. And thank you, Jesus.

Everything's gonna be alright!

Finally, my brothers [and sisters], rejoice in the Lord.

That was the day I learned to rejoice in the Lord.

Can I get a witness?

The Prayer

Abba Father, we thank you for your Son, Jesus, who for the joy before him endured the cross, scorning its shame, and sat down at your right hand where he shall reign forevermore. Teach us joy through the faith of rejoicing. Teach us to sing in a way that transcends mere song. Thank you for your ever-present willingness to make your joy our joy. We pray in Jesus' name, amen.

The Questions

- What do you make of this depiction of joy as transcending emotion and coming as a fruit of learning to rejoice?
- We don't rejoice because we have joy, we rejoice because we seek joy. What do you think of that?
- How do you think of the difference between joy and happiness, and how have you seen those two things differently in your own experience?

When Passing the Test Is a Big, Fat Fail

29

PHILIPPIANS 3:4B–6 | If someone else thinks they have reasons to put confidence in the flesh, I have more: circumcised on the eighth day, of the people of Israel, of the tribe of Benjamin, a Hebrew of Hebrews; in regard to the law, a Pharisee; as for zeal, persecuting the church; as for righteousness based on the law, faultless.

Consider This

About those blasted Judaizers. You thought we skipped them, didn't you? I got so carried away with joy I failed to make reference to the larger portion of yesterday's Scripture text. Paul actually broke into some good old-fashioned apostolic name-calling: "Watch out for those dogs, those evildoers, those mutilators of the flesh" (v. 2).

There are layers of irony wrapped up in those particular names alone, but we must move on. Judaizers were those Jewish Christians who believed that in order to become a follower of Jesus one had to keep pretty strict adherence to the Mosaic law, most notably circumcision. Paul was not having it. There is a huge backstory here that culminated in what we today call the Jerusalem Council, which can be read about in Acts 15. The breakthrough bottom line held that a person didn't have to first become a Jew in order to become a Christian.

The Christian faith is not an outside-in deal. It is inside-out. Salvation is by grace through faith alone, Paul said, so that no one could boast (Eph. 2:8–9). And, of all people, Paul could have been the chief boaster. Today he rolls out his religious résumé. Tomorrow he will run it through the shredder. Paul passed the test. He got an A+ only to realize it was all a big, fat fail. And he glories in it. Just wow!

If someone else thinks they have reasons to put confidence in the flesh, I have more: circumcised on the eighth day, of the people of Israel, of the tribe of Benjamin, a Hebrew of Hebrews; in regard to the law, a Pharisee; as for zeal, persecuting the church; as for righteousness based on the law, faultless.

The gospel is Jesus plus absolutely, utterly, and completely nothing else. It doesn't matter how bad you've been or how good you are. Whether Jew or Gentile, everyone enters on the same terms. Circumcision, the thing that would have meant everything to Paul, now means less than nothing. Even more astonishing is the way Paul completely changes the meaning of circumcision from an outward sign to an inward reality: "For it is we who are the circumcision, we who serve God by his Spirit, who boast in Christ Jesus, and who put no confidence in the flesh" (Phil. 3:3).

The gospel of Jesus Christ is simultaneously the most exclusive and the most inclusive offer in the universe. Total exclusivity: there is only one way by which human beings can be saved—by grace through faith in the atoning work of Jesus Christ on the cross. "Nothing but the blood of Jesus," as the old standard sings. Total inclusivity: anyone can be saved—all who will repent of their sin and place their trust in Jesus

Christ. No one is unqualified or disqualified. In fact, because of the prevenient grace of God, everyone is prequalified. The free grace of God has, in essence, freed the will of the human race to make a decision to trust Christ. But everyone must decide.

This is why we brag on Jesus alone. This is why we boast in the cross alone. This is why everything that mattered so much to Paul before doesn't matter at all anymore. This is the only freedom. Everything else is just another form of slavery.

With Jesus there is no more trying to measure up. The gospel only measures down.

The Prayer

Abba Father, we thank you for your Son, Jesus, who is able to save us completely by no merit of our own but by his grace. Give us the grace to even grasp grace and to know that our everything is still nothing when it comes to measuring up to the glory of God. Open our eyes to the glorious truth that God will give us everything in exchange for our nothing if we can let go of our everything in order to be embraced by grace alone. We pray in Jesus' name, amen.

The Questions

- So, let me be blunt. Are you saved? Are you ready to measure down?
- Are you in touch with your own deep need to measure up in life? If you are trying to measure up in every other area of your life, how could you possibly not be trying to also measure up with God?
- Is grace going deeper in you, or are you still striving after it?

30 Have You Seen My Spiritual Merit Badge Collection?

PHILIPPIANS 3:7–9 | But whatever were gains to me I now consider loss for the sake of Christ. What is more, I consider everything a loss because of the surpassing worth of knowing Christ Jesus my Lord, for whose sake I have lost all things. I consider them garbage, that I may gain Christ and be found in him, not having a righteousness of my own that comes from the law, but that which is through faith in Christ—the righteousness that comes from God on the basis of faith.

Consider This

Do you have a merit badge mentality?

I remember being in the Boy Scouts and the quest to amass merit badges. If you wanted to advance in the ranks of scouting, you had to earn merit badges. Like young soldiers, we longed to decorate ourselves with these marks of our achievement. They were markers of status and prestige and sources of pride, and all of that was just fine for the Boy Scout phase of my life.

You will remember from yesterday's text how a group of Jewish Christians (the Judaizers) wanted to require non-Jewish people (the Gentiles) to earn a host of merit badges (keeping the Mosaic law, namely circumcision) before they could become bona fide Christians. Paul would not have it, and you will remember how he essentially pulled out his own collection of merit badges (a.k.a. his bona fides) and put them on display. Well, today, he all but throws them in the trash.

What happened? Paul met Jesus, and he never got over it. He met the one for whom he had longed. Once we see the treasure of Jesus, our trophies so pale in comparison we regard them as trash.

Permit me a little latitude to make an observation. Like many of you, I am well past any shred of illusion that my merit badges can earn me even the slightest modicum of salvation. What troubles me is my merit badge mentality on this side of the cross.

Years ago I found myself in a spiritual retreat setting with a group of men I had never met. We all knew each other had to be "somebody" in order to even be present in the group. In no time, all of us were finding ways to humbly let each other know of our Christian merit badges. On one hand we all knew we were miserable sinners who had been saved by grace alone (and we even had a way of turning that into a merit badge of sorts), but after that we had all done pretty well at distinguishing ourselves as super-Christians. I will never forget the retreat leader's first words to the group. He said, "It's time to take off your spiritual badges. They need to be checked at the door." We all knew exactly what he meant, and I have been trying to take mine off ever since.

Something in me, and I suspect in you, doesn't want to just shine; I want to outshine. I want you to know who I am for Jesus and what I've done for Jesus and how I've lived for Jesus. I want to show you my merit badges. I want to be admired and appreciated and affirmed. Compare this to Paul's words:

But whatever were gains to me I now consider loss for the sake of Christ. What is more, I consider everything a loss because of the surpassing worth of knowing Christ Jesus my Lord, for whose sake I have lost all things. I consider them garbage, that I may gain Christ and be found in him.

Paul wanted us to know who Jesus was for him and what Jesus had done for him and how Jesus lived in him. He wanted to show us Jesus' merit badge: the cross. He wanted Jesus to be admired and appreciated and affirmed.

There's a great story about Saint Thomas Aquinas, a thirteenth-century priest, scholar, and doctor of the church. One of the most prolific and influential theologians in history, he had written more than one hundred books, treatises, and theological documents by the time he was fifty. On December 6, the Feast Day of Saint Nicholas, in the year 1273, he was celebrating the Eucharist in the Chapel of Saint Nicholas in Naples, Italy, when he had an encounter with God from which he never recovered. He was writing his magnum opus at the time, *Summa Theologica*. Though not complete, it amounted to some thirty-eight treatises, three thousand articles, and ten thousand objections. After this encounter he refused to ever write again. In response to his secretary's urging, he famously said, "Reginald, I can do no more. The end of my labors has come. Such things have been revealed to me that all I have written seems as so much straw."*

The surpassing worth of knowing Christ Jesus my Lord . . .

The Prayer

Abba Father, we thank you for your Son, Jesus, whom to know is to love and whom to love is to live. Come, Holy Spirit, and open the eyes of our hearts to grasp the surpassing worth of knowing Christ Jesus our Lord and then to see the paltry collection of merit badges we once considered gain. Shake us free from our illusions about ourselves that we might see the true vision of Jesus and find ourselves alive in him alone. We pray in Jesus' name, amen.

The Questions

- What is it about you that wants others to see your collection of spiritual merit badges?
- Where are you in your grasping of the surpassing worth of knowing Christ Jesus your Lord and being found in him with a righteousness you had nothing to do with?
- Why is it we think we must be justified by grace but don't grasp that we will only be sanctified by grace in the same way—Jesus only, Jesus ever?

How did you come to know Jesus?
What is your ministry?
"   " the hardest thing in your life?

---

* Quoted in Hank Hanegraaff, *Truth Matters, Life Matters More: The Unexpected Beauty of an Authentic Christian Life* (Nashville, TN: W Publishing, 2019), xxxiii.

31 The Meaninglessness of Resurrection without Death

PHILIPPIANS 3:10–11 ESV | [T]hat I may know him and the power of his resurrection, and may share his sufferings, becoming like him in his death, that by any means possible I may attain the resurrection from the dead.

Consider This

This one is a "rememberizer."

There are places in Scripture, passages and even single verses, that capture the essence of the whole Bible. They distill thousands of words into a sentence or two, and, in doing so, they capture essence and purpose and even passion. This is one of those texts. I share it below in the particular version in which I rememberized it:

"I want to know Christ and the power of his resurrection and the fellowship of sharing in his sufferings, becoming like him in his death, and so, somehow, to attain to the resurrection from the dead" (NIV 1984).

It does not begin with "I should," or "I ought to," or "I need," or "I wish," or "I think." It says, "I want," which lands us in the realm of longing and desire and deep will.

Note also it does not say I want to know "about" Christ. This is not mere knowing for knowledge's sake. This is the knowing of deep personal relationship, the knowing of deep calling to deep.

So what does this entail? It can't mean whatever we want it to mean. In the last chapter Paul gave us the resplendent vision of the mind of Christ. Remember the V pattern? Paul makes very clear in the next several words exactly what it means to know Christ: (1) knowing the power of his resurrection; (2) sharing in the fellowship of his sufferings; (3) becoming like him in his death; and (4) the resurrection of the body at the end of the age and life, life, and more life for all the ages to come.

We are all for a big yes to numbers 1 and 4. Numbers 2 and 3 can be another story. We mistakenly think of resurrection as numbers 1 and 4 and of the cross as numbers 2 and 3. The cross is the whole thing. The cross is the movement of death and resurrection. We do not get one without the other. There is no knowing Jesus apart from the cross, which means there is no knowing Jesus apart from the grand movement of death and resurrection. What does resurrection even mean apart from death?

Let me repeat, there is no knowing the power of his resurrection without sharing in the fellowship of his suffering and becoming like him in his death. To borrow Thomas à Kempis's phrase, this is the "royal way of the holy cross."

One more thing. Participating in his sufferings and becoming like him in his death is not a grit-your-teeth-and-bear-it kind of experience. It is the journey of learning to love like God loves. In fact, this is the core essence of discipleship to Jesus: the way of the cross, the way of the great love.

The Prayer

Abba Father, we thank you for your Son, Jesus, who is himself the perfect embodiment of the love of God. We want to know this love, which is to say we want to know him. Lead us in this way of the cross, this path of death and resurrection, all the days of our lives. We pray in Jesus' name, amen.

The Questions

- Have you ever thought of the cross as both death and resurrection? Does this make sense to you?
- How are you growing in your understanding of sharing in the fellowship of Christ's sufferings? What does this mean to you?
- "I want to know Christ." On a scale of 1 to 10 (with 10 being the highest value), where do you scale yourself?

32   If Your Faith Were a Game, How Would You Play It?

PHILIPPIANS 3:12–14 ESV | Not that I have already obtained this or am already perfect, but I press on to make it my own, because Christ Jesus has made me his own. Brothers, I do not consider that I have made it my own. But one thing I do: forgetting what lies behind and straining forward to what lies ahead,

I press on toward the goal for the prize of the upward call of God in Christ Jesus.

Consider This

What if we gamified our faith?

"But wait," you say, "what is gamification?" Thanks for asking. According to Wikipedia, gamification is "the application of game-design elements and game principles in non-game contexts." Fitness is an area brimming with gamification these days (e.g., Fitbit).

Paul often employs athletic metaphors to talk about faith, but I think it was more than just metaphor for Paul. He lived in the metaphor, and to that degree he gamified it. In addition to today's text consider these examples:

> "And then I will be able to boast on the day of Christ that I did not run or labor in vain." (Phil. 2:16b)

> "I wanted to be sure I was not running and had not been running my race in vain." (Gal. 2:2b)

> "I have fought the good fight, I have finished the race, I have kept the faith." (2 Tim. 4:7)

> "Similarly, anyone who competes as an athlete does not receive the victor's crown except by competing according to the rules." (2 Tim. 2:5)

> "Do you not know that in a race all the runners run, but only one gets the prize? Run in such a way as to

get the prize. Everyone who competes in the games goes into strict training. They do it to get a crown that will not last, but we do it to get a crown that will last forever." (1 Cor. 9:24–25)

"Therefore, since we are surrounded by such a great cloud of witnesses, let us throw off everything that hinders and the sin that so easily entangles. And let us run with perseverance the race marked out for us." (Heb. 12:1)

See my point? Far more than an instructional metaphor for Paul, he lived out his faith through these lenses. He thought like a gamer, applying game principles in a non-game context. It was no longer about religious rule-keeping for Paul. It was about winning the race and claiming the prize. Paul was, as the saying goes, "in it to win it."

Here's the interesting thing about games: games require exacting skill and tremendous focus; at the same time, games create enormous contexts of grace. As the saying goes, "You win some. You lose some. And some get rained out." With a game you can forget what is past and press on to the next contest. In fact, you must. As soon as you complete one challenge or win one game, there's another one in front of you. With a gamer mentality you are always training for the next race or contest. And what's the secret to becoming a champion? Practice, practice, practice, right?

In the present day I hear a lot about Christian practices, but not too much on the concept of practice. Maybe the reason why is we have lost sight of the next big game coming up.

Who is ready to play?

The Prayer

Abba Father, we thank you for your Son, Jesus, our great champion, who shows us what it looks like to be the ultimate winner through an apparent ultimate loss. Teach us that because of your win, we cannot lose. May your grace set us free to let go of the past, and may your Spirit fill us with courage and power to press on and go for the win. That's how we want to play it, Lord. We pray in Jesus' name, amen.

The Questions

- What do you think of this notion of approaching the Christian faith through the lens of gamification?
- How might your marriage change if you brought faith into a gamification mentality? What would winning look like? How about forgetting what is behind and pressing on toward the mark?
- Could this gamification approach we see so consistently with Paul help us to take ourselves less seriously that we might take the game more seriously?

Growing Churches That Don't Grow People

33

PHILIPPIANS 3:15–16 | All of us, then, who are mature should take such a view of things. And if on some point you think differently, that too God will make clear to you. Only let us live up to what we have already attained.

Consider This

Mature. It's a word we don't really get too well. We see movies advertised for "mature audiences," which presumably means children shouldn't see it but it's okay for adults because they have already seen it all. They make dog food for mature dogs, which means they are old.

When Paul says "mature," he uses the Greek word *teleios*. In studying the Bible we can get a fuller sense of how a writer is using a term by seeing how and where he uses it in other places in the Bible and also how other speakers or writers use the term. That's where this gets interesting. This little word, *teleios,* is used by Jesus in one of the most challenging texts in all of Scripture: "Be perfect, therefore, as your heavenly Father is perfect" (Matt. 5:48).

To be perfect does not mean perfection as we commonly think of the term. It means to be mature, possessed by a love of another magnitude of order—the very love of God.

Hear Paul in his letter to the Hebrews: "Therefore let us move beyond the elementary teachings about Christ and be taken forward to maturity, not laying again the foundation of repentance from acts that lead to death, and of faith in God" (Heb. 6:1).

And to the Ephesians: "until we all reach unity in the faith and in the knowledge of the Son of God and become mature, attaining to the whole measure of the fullness of Christ" (Eph. 4:13).

And to the Corinthians: "We do, however, speak a message of wisdom among the mature, but not the wisdom of this age or of the rulers of this age, who are coming to nothing" (1 Cor. 2:6.).

We could go on and cite references to the Romans and the Colossians and the Galatians and so on. You get the point. Paul did not measure church growth by numbers. He measured it by maturity.

We mostly get it backward today. Our primary question is: How do we grow the church? The real question is: How does the Holy Spirit grow people? As a consequence, we have nearly mastered the art of growing churches that don't grow people. We get people busy in all manner of Christian activity, but when it comes to measuring the maturity of people, we have no metrics. And, as they say, we manage what we measure.

What if, instead of asking how we get people to come to church or how we get people to come back or how we get people involved or assimilated or tithing or in a home group or in Sunday school or going on a mission trip or what we want people to know . . . what if we asked much deeper questions, the kinds of questions Jesus might ask? Who do we want people to become? How would we know if we became it? What are the markers of mature faith? Who in our midst shows forth the qualities of perfect love in their lives?

I've said it before and I won't stop saying it, but the primary reason we are arrested in our maturity is we don't have the kinds of relationships it takes to grow us into maturity. Mature faith and character simply do not happen alone. I would love for you to dialogue about this in your bands today and in our Facebook group. By the way, if you haven't joined the Facebook group and you are a Facebook person, give it a shot. Good conversations are happening there.

The Prayer

Abba Father, we thank you for your Son, Jesus, who is the exact image of God, the perfect representation of your being in human form. His life shows us what a real mature human being actually is, and your Spirit makes it possible for us to live as such. Shake us free from our crowd-based, self-satisfied mediocrity. We want to be a real Christians. We pray in Jesus' name, amen.

The Questions

- How do you define the marks of mature and maturing faith?
- Who do you think of as a mature follower of Jesus? What makes that so?
- On a scale of 1 to 10 (with 1 being infantile and 10 being saintly), where do you place yourself on the spectrum, and what words would you use to classify it?

34 The Difference between Supermodels and Saints

PHILIPPIANS 3:17–19 | Join together in following my example, brothers and sisters, and just as you have us as a model, keep your eyes on those who live as we do. For, as I have often told you before and now tell you again even with tears, many live as enemies of the cross of Christ. Their destiny is destruction, their god is their stomach, and their glory is in their shame. Their mind is set on earthly things.

Consider This

Have you ever thought of the apostle Paul as a supermodel? I haven't either, until now. We typically think of supermodels as tall, rail-thin, beautiful women wearing clothing made by leading fashion designers whose picture is on every fashion magazine in the world at the same time. They tend to create highly unrealistic examples for our daughters to pattern their own appearances and self-image after.

Okay, so maybe Paul wasn't actually a supermodel after all, but he did say to follow his example. That's what models do. They give us something to pattern after. The New Testament has a different kind of word for supermodel. The word is *hagios* in Greek. It means "holy one" or "saint."

Whereas the idea of a supermodel is all about maintaining a flawless outward appearance, the notion of a saint centers on a deep internal magnificence. It manifests not through appearance but by the quality of radiance in one's character and the depth of love in one's relationships. When Paul calls on us to live as examples of Christ, he is talking about a way of life that points not to us, but a life through which Jesus Christ reveals himself. Paul is not talking about being religious but becoming holy.

I like the way Albert Day speaks of holiness: "True holiness is a witness that cannot be ignored. Real sainthood is a phenomenon to which even the worldling pays tribute. The power of a life, where Christ is exalted, would arrest and subdue those who are bored to tears by our thin version of Christianity and wholly uninterested in mere churchmanship."*

We need more saints on earth, not just in heaven. We need more ordinary saints, not just the exceptional, unreachable exemplars. Why? Because there are too many counterexamples. Hear Paul's deep grief on this point:

For, as I have often told you before and now tell you again even with tears, many live as enemies of the cross of Christ. Their destiny is destruction, their god is their stomach, and their glory is in their shame. Their mind is set on earthly things.

He is not talking about pagans here but some so-called followers of Jesus. They are compromised Christians. He is likely referencing leaders who claimed the name of Christ but defied the mind of Christ and the lifestyle of a Christian. The word *indulgent* comes to mind.

Then and now, Christian leaders, often well-intentioned, will compromise with the agendas of the culture and the interests of the world in the interest of preserving relationship or unity and in the name of Christian love. Such leaders become unwitting enemies of the cross of Christ. Indeed, love covers a multitude of sins (1 Peter 4:8), yet it never indulges

---

* Albert Edward Day, *Discipline and Discovery* (Upper Room, 1947), n.p.

sin. The moment love compromises with sin it ceases to be love and begins its journey toward becoming license.

It's why we speak a lot in our work of holy love, which demonstrates extraordinary compassion for sinners while refusing to compromise with sin. Love cannot indulge sin because compromising with sin means being complicit in the strategy of sin, which is to destroy people. Love is incompatible with sin, not because love is good and sin is bad, but because love heals and sin destroys.

If I'm honest, what inclines me to make public compromises with sinners are my own private compromises with sin. This is why I must become more mature in my understanding and life of love. Sin is so seductive and its strategies can seem so reasonable. In fact, sin is so deceptive as to make standing against it seem not only humanly unreasonable but culturally untenable, not only unloving but insensitive.

Let's help each other become mature, coming to fullness in Christ and even perfection in love. Holiness is the deep internal magnificence we long for.

The Prayer

Abba Father, we thank you for your Son, Jesus, who by the cross has atoned for our sin and robbed sin of its power over us. Forgive us for our compromises with sin and even more for the way our indulgence leads us to places where we will regard sin as not sin. Thank you that the gospel will not reason with sin. Awaken us to an arresting holiness that overpowers sin and reveals the beautiful holy love of Jesus. We pray in Jesus' name, amen.

The Questions

- Are you willing to put your life and faith forward as an example to be followed?
- Why do we think that it would be prideful or pious to do this? Do you see how this refusal can be a smoke screen for our own spiritual laziness?
- Where are you living as an enemy of the cross of Christ? Where are you needing to mature?

35 | Dueling Citizenships

PHILIPPIANS 3:20–21 | But our citizenship is in heaven. And we eagerly await a Savior from there, the Lord Jesus Christ, who, by the power that enables him to bring everything under his control, will transform our lowly bodies so that they will be like his glorious body.

Consider This

But our citizenship is in heaven.

I once heard an unusual message from Gary Haugen, the head of the International Justice Mission. I expected to hear a talk on child slavery or genocide or sex trafficking—areas where he has provided heroic service around the world. Instead, he spoke on citizenship. His basic message: our most powerful asset is our American citizenship. He made a compelling case for the great power we possess as individuals simply by virtue of our United States citizenship and of the responsibility we bear to steward it with great care. I honestly had never thought about it before. I assumed it, taking the benefits, powers, privileges, and responsibilities for granted.

Paul would have felt this way about his Roman citizenship. As America is now, so Rome was in his day—the most powerful nation on earth. Philippi was a Roman colony that would have been a big deal to its residents. They would have stood and beamed with great pride as the ancient equivalent of Lee Greenwood's "God Bless the U.S.A." came over the loudspeakers.

I love America. I think it's the greatest nation on earth . . .

But our citizenship is in heaven.

All the followers of Jesus have dual citizenship. The question we must ask ourselves is: Which citizenship will be primary for me? Am I an American Christian or will I be a Christian American? See the difference? I love America, but the longer I live, the more I realize that in order to really love America, I need to love Jesus more.

The greatest power in my possession and my greatest stewardship is not my American citizenship (though I value this). It is my citizenship in heaven.

But our citizenship is in heaven.

I love the way Paul puts this in Hebrews 11:

> People who say such things show that they are looking
> for a country of their own. If they had been thinking

of the country they had left, they would have had opportunity to return. Instead, they were longing for a better country—a heavenly one. Therefore God is not ashamed to be called their God, for he has prepared a city for them. (vv. 14–16)

The Prayer

Abba Father, we thank you for your Son, Jesus, who is the King of heaven and earth. He is Lord. Sift our commitments and order our loyalties. We want to be real Christians. We pray in Jesus' name, amen.

The Questions

- American Christian or Christian American—what's the difference?
- Why does it matter?
- How do you steward your American citizenship (if you are an American)? How do you steward your heavenly citizenship?

36 Why Unity without Like-Mindedness Is Not Unity

PHILIPPIANS 4:1–3 | Therefore, my brothers and sisters, you whom I love and long for, my joy and crown, stand firm in the Lord in this way, dear friends!

I plead with Euodia and I plead with Syntyche to be of the same mind in the Lord. Yes, and I ask you, my true companion, help these women since they have contended at my side in the cause of the gospel, along with Clement and the rest of my co-workers, whose names are in the book of life.

Consider This

How would you like to be Euodia and Syntyche—immortalized forever as those two women who got called out by Paul in the Bible, no less? Their names are on the board with a checkmark for all eternity to come!

Here's what I find interesting: Paul is not asking them to get along despite their differences. He's asking them to "be of the same mind in the Lord." He could have said, "Stop arguing about this doctrine or that theological issue. It is more important that you get along and be united than it is to be of the same mind."

There is a way of being unified that is not unity at all. There is a way of getting along in so-called Christian community that makes a mockery of Christian community. Is it more loving to paper over differences for the sake of unity or to own the inability to achieve like-mindedness, work toward mutual respect, and pursue different visions and futures?

It bears repeating. Paul's goal, as the planter and overseer of churches, is not unity but like-mindedness, not latitudinarianism but love. Remember his earlier word to the Philippians:

Therefore if you have any encouragement from being united with Christ, if any comfort from his love, if any

> common sharing in the Spirit, if any tenderness and
> compassion, then make my joy complete by being
> like-minded, having the same love, being one in spirit
> and of one mind. (Phil. 2:1–2)

Like-minded, same love, one in spirit, of one mind. It strikes me that in the midst of conflict, the remedy is not unity at the expense of like-mindedness. The remedy is to pursue like-mindedness. Even more important is the source of our alignment. Republicans and Democrats will never align around core convictions and vision. They see the world from two very disparate points of view. The best that can be hoped for is some form of compromise.

Christians, on the other hand, must pursue like-mindedness not around their own disparate opinions but around the Word of God. Where divergent interpretations of Scripture cannot be reconciled, both parties must own this. In pursuing like-mindedness, what is most needed is the mind of Christ. Neither should be expected to abandon their conviction in the interest of unity, for it would not be unity at all. It is better to pursue separate visions with mutual respect and some modicum of love, which itself can be harmonizing despite the disparateness, than to live in open disagreement and defiance of one another while calling it unity.

The Prayer

Abba Father, we thank you for your Son, Jesus, who prayed that we would all be one just as you are one. Thank you that this is your work to accomplish, not ours. Thank you for calling us to pursue like-mindedness around your Word. Give us a humility that becomes the mind of Christ, that we might learn to love others the way you love them. We pray in Jesus' name, amen.

The Questions

- Do you tend to agree or disagree with today's reflection on unity and like-mindedness?
- Why are people willing to compromise on conviction in order to achieve unity?
- How do you see the difference between pursuing unity and pursuing like-mindedness?

What to Do in Times of Trouble (Part One)

37

PHILIPPIANS 4:4–5 | Rejoice in the Lord always. I will say it again: Rejoice! Let your gentleness be evident to all. The Lord is near.

Consider This

You will remember some days back we addressed Paul's extraordinary emphasis on joy. He uses the term some sixteen times in this letter from a Roman prison cell. Let me cite a portion of what I wrote prior:

Joy is not happiness. It's not a feeling or an emotion. Joy is not positive thinking. Joy is a fruit of the Holy Spirit (Gal. 5:22–23). Joy is supernatural. It is a wellness that transcends health, a state of being that eclipses emotion, and an inner realism that overwhelms apparent reality. Though it transcends the ephemeral notion of earthly emotion, we might think of joy as the primary emotion of the realm of eternal reality. Joy is that deep inner conviction that though things are not right everything is going to be alright. Joy is experienced by those who exercise their faith through rejoicing.

Paul brings tremendous emphasis to this point: "Rejoice in the Lord always." When we explore the Greek text, we find the meaning of this term, *always*, means always! There is no circumstance in life that can elude joy. While joy comes from the Holy Spirit, it comes to those who will choose, by faith, to rejoice. In case he was not clear, he repeats it: "I will say it again: Rejoice!"

Tomorrow we will deal with Paul's admonition to "not be anxious about anything" (v. 6). In between these two words of instruction comes a third: "Let your gentleness be evident to all" (v. 5a). When hard situations and difficult circumstances come our way, anxiety is the natural human reaction. Fear so easily takes root in the frail and broken human spirit. In fact, the only thing stronger than fear is the love of God. Always remember, "Perfect love casts out fear" (1 John 4:18 ESV). Fear produces anxiety. So what is the antidote to anxiety? Peace? Well, yes, but what is the pathway to peace? The answer may surprise you. It's gentleness.

So what does joy have to do with gentleness? Joy is the surprising manifestation of the presence of God in the midst of difficult circumstances. To rejoice means to declare the confounding presence of God to your circumstances. There is truth in the cliché "Don't tell your God how big your problems are. Tell your problems how big your God is."

Let's listen to the way James speaks of rejoicing. He no sooner says hello in his message than he says this, "Consider it pure joy, my brothers and sisters, whenever you face trials of many kinds, because you know that the testing of your faith produces perseverance. Let perseverance finish its work so that you may be mature and complete, not lacking anything" (James 1:2–4).

There are two kinds of people in the world: those facing hard circumstances and those who will soon be facing hard circumstances. Jesus made it clear when he stated the obvious, "In this world you will have trouble," but then he gave us cause for rejoicing when he added, "but take heart! I have overcome the world" (John 16:33b).

In the face of trouble we have two basic choices: anxiety or rejoicing. If we do not choose to rejoice, we effectively choose anxiety. It's why Paul is so emphatic. Like James, he is not giving us a suggestion but a command:

Rejoice in the Lord always. I will say it again: Rejoice!

The Prayer

Abba Father, we thank you for your Son, Jesus, who for the joy set before him endured the cross. We confess so often in the face of hardships and trials we do not rejoice. We retreat into self-pity and even despair. Come, Holy Spirit, and teach us to rejoice instead. This way is foreign to us. We need your help. We pray in Jesus' name, amen.

The Questions

- Why is it hard for you to rejoice in the face of trials and difficulties?
- What does it look like to rejoice? Practically speaking, how might you do it?
- What do you make of these connections between joy and anxiety, and gentleness and peace?

38 | What to Do in Times of Trouble (Part Two)

PHILIPPIANS 4:6–7 | Do not be anxious about anything, but in every situation, by prayer and petition, with thanksgiving, present your requests to God. And the peace of God, which transcends all understanding, will guard your hearts and your minds in Christ Jesus.

Consider This

Rejoicing in the face of trials and difficult circumstances leads to a surprising countenance in the spirit of the one rejoicing: gentleness. Just as anxiety and all the harshness it brings is contagious, so is gentleness. Gentleness, remember, is a fruit of the Holy Spirit (Gal. 5:22–23). It is the supernatural disposition of a person who knows deep down the Lord is near (Phil. 4:5b). Though he blazes with the brilliance of ten thousand suns, he whispers.

It's why Paul wants us to let our gentleness "be evident to all" (Phil. 4:5a). Gentleness is a prerequisite to peace. The peace of God is the presence of God, and, though he be near, he can still be far from our perception and experience.

There's a powerful story in 2 Kings about the prophet Elisha in the midst of a dire situation. Because of Elisha's strong help to the king of Israel, the king of Aram pursued him to death.

> Then he sent horses and chariots and a strong force there. They went by night and surrounded the city.
>
> When the servant of the man of God got up and went out early the next morning, an army with horses and chariots had surrounded the city. "Oh no, my lord! What shall we do?" the servant asked.
>
> "Don't be afraid," the prophet answered. "Those who are with us are more than those who are with them."
>
> And Elisha prayed, "Open his eyes, Lord, so that he may see." Then the Lord opened the servant's eyes, and he looked and saw the hills full of horses and chariots of fire all around Elisha. (2 Kings 6:14–17)

To rejoice in the face of trial is to swing the ax at the base of the tree of anxiety. A gentle spirit and disposition has a way of pushing back the borders of difficult circumstances and creating space for a different kind of response: prayer.

Do not be anxious about anything, but in every situation, by prayer and petition, with thanksgiving, present your requests to God.

Prayer and petition with thanksgiving is not frantic, frenetic prayer. So often we worry our prayers, which can be another way of expressing our anxiety. Prayer and petition with thanksgiving means we must get out of praying in our heads and put our prayers into tangible, spoken language. Our prayers need to be more than thoughts. The importance of forming our prayers into audible words cannot be understated. Remember, in the faith of the Bible, words create worlds.

All of this paves the way for something genuinely new to happen:

And the peace of God, which transcends all understanding, will guard your hearts and your minds in Christ Jesus.

Sometimes circumstances change. Sometimes they do not. It's why we will soon hear Paul say, "I know what it is to be in need, and I know what it is to have plenty. I have learned the secret of being content in any and every situation, whether well fed or hungry, whether living in plenty or in want" (Phil. 4:12). It brings to mind the celebrated hymn "It Is Well with My Soul."

> When peace like a river attendeth my way,
> when sorrows like sea billows roll;

whatever my lot, thou hast taught me to say,
"It is well, it is well with my soul."*

Let's set up camp and pitch our tent here for today.

The Prayer

Abba Father, we thank you for your Son, Jesus, who not only gives us his peace but who is himself our peace. Come, Holy Spirit, and reveal our anxieties to us; surface it that it might be enveloped and evaporated by the peace of God. Lord Jesus Christ, come closer than our anxieties and guard our hearts and minds. We pray in Jesus' name, amen.

The Questions

- Do you tend to be more harsh or gentle with yourself?
- Could this harshness cloak anxiety just under the surface of your life? What would it look like to become attuned to your anxiety?
- Rejoicing is not a denial of our circumstances, but a faith-filled way of presenting our circumstances to God. How will the manner and language of your praying change in response to Paul's teaching?

---

* "It Is Well with My Soul," Horatio Gates Spafford, 1873. Public domain.

39 The Problem with Stinking Thinking and What to Do about It

PHILIPPIANS 4:8 | Finally, brothers and sisters, whatever is true, whatever is noble, whatever is right, whatever is pure, whatever is lovely, whatever is admirable—if anything is excellent or praiseworthy—think about such things.

Consider This

Today's text often gets taken out of its context and put on refrigerator magnets, bumper stickers, and all manner of sit-arounds.

Finally, brothers and sisters, whatever is true, whatever is noble, whatever is right, whatever is pure, whatever is lovely, whatever is admirable—if anything is excellent or praiseworthy—think about such things.

I suppose this text is helpful in any context, but it will serve us to remember the context in which Paul writes it: difficult circumstances, trials, and hardships. Our thoughts and patterns of thinking have a way of setting us up for success or failure.

Proverbs 23 famously says, "For as he thinks in his heart, so is he" (v. 7a NKJV). Though the source is disputed, the following quote, attributed to Frank Outlaw, captures profound wisdom:

> Watch your thoughts, they become words;
> watch your words, they become actions;
> watch your actions, they become habits;
> watch your habits, they become character;
> watch your character, for it becomes your destiny.

The force of the quote is this: our thoughts become our destiny.

Do we want our destiny to be true, noble, right, pure, lovely, admirable, excellent, and praiseworthy? Of course we do. I don't know about you, but my thinking needs work. In the recovery community, they have a condition they call "stinking thinking." Sometimes you will hear it said, "Stinking thinking leads to drinking." My thinking, left to itself, will turn toward negativity. I can get down on myself and on others and on life in general. It is like someone in my brain is slowly dimming the lights, causing my vision to become constricted until I can barely see what is right in front of me. It leads to a type of depression akin to a low-grade fever. It's just there, quietly handicapping everything I do. I know a lot of you struggle in this same way.

Bringing it full circle, these ways of stinking thinking are death to joy. Remember where this whole conversation began? "Rejoice in the Lord always. I will say it again: Rejoice!" (Phil. 4:4).

What if I thought of my mind as a garden? I would want to plant good things there. I would want to stay on top of the weeding, uprooting negative thoughts as they emerged above the ground, not letting them take root and spread. I would pay attention to cultivating my thought life and nourishing it with fresh water and, yes, more weeding.

The Prayer

Abba Father, we thank you for your Son, Jesus, who shows us what it looks like to set our minds and hearts on things above. Come, Holy Spirit, and claim the space of our thought lives that our minds might be a place of glorious light in the Lord. We pray in Jesus' name, amen.

The Questions

- How do you intentionally sow the true, noble, pure, admirable, and so forth into your thought life?
- In what particular ways are you prone to stinking thinking?
- What might weeding look like in the garden of your mind? How can you catch the weeds at the earliest point?

40 The Great Differentiator

PHILIPPIANS 4:9 ESV | What you have learned and received and heard and seen in me—practice these things, and the God of peace will be with you.

Consider This

It's not enough to learn or receive or hear or see. It must be put into practice.

So let me ask you the hard question: What are you putting into practice? If you are anything like me, it's easy to read something, think about it, ponder it, enjoy it, be challenged by it, agree with it for the most part, register an intention to do something about it, and then check e-mail, send a few text messages, get busy doing other things, and all of a sudden it's already tomorrow and the process repeats itself. I know it's like that for me as the writer, so I can only imagine how it must be as the reader.

Now let me ask you an even harder question: What two or three things are you actively putting into practice from our journey through Philippians so far? We have covered a lot of ground, and I know I've thrown a lot at you. It's impossible to put into practice all that has been discussed. That's the problem with the so-much-ness of it all. Because we can't do everything, it's hard to know what to do or to decide what matters most. We don't intend to not do anything about what we are reading, but we are on a planet that is moving at 67,000 miles per hour, and that's before we even get out of bed. It's just easier to learn, receive, hear, and see stuff in God's Word, which takes effort in itself. It's a lot harder to sustain practice.

So because I love you, I'm going to remind you of the truth you already know. All of the learning and receiving and hearing and seeing in the world will amount to less than nothing if we do not put it into practice. Hear Brother James on this point:

> Do not merely listen to the word, and so deceive your-selves. Do what it says. Anyone who listens to the word

but does not do what it says is like someone who looks at his face in a mirror and, after looking at himself, goes away and immediately forgets what he looks like. But whoever looks intently into the perfect law that gives freedom, and continues in it—not forgetting what they have heard, but doing it—they will be blessed in what they do. (James 1:22–25)

Let's give Jimmy's brother, our Lord Jesus Christ, the last word on the topic today:

"Therefore everyone who hears these words of mine and puts them into practice is like a wise man who built his house on the rock. The rain came down, the streams rose, and the winds blew and beat against that house; yet it did not fall, because it had its foundation on the rock. But everyone who hears these words of mine and does not put them into practice is like a foolish man who built his house on sand. The rain came down, the streams rose, and the winds blew and beat against that house, and it fell with a great crash." (Matt. 7:24–27)

Catch the difference between the house that withstood the storm and the one that crashed? One word: *practice.* It is the great differentiator.

The Prayer

Abba Father, we thank you for your Son, Jesus, who is the Word made flesh, the perfect embodiment of your ways and your will. He is the one who shows us how practice makes perfect, for he is himself the perfect practice of your Word. We want to be like Jesus. Grant us the simplicity of a long, slow, simple obedience in the same direction. We pray in Jesus' name, amen.

The Questions

- What one thing from our time in Philippians so far are you trying to put into practice? (For me, it's learning to rejoice in the face of hardship.)
- Do you ever have the mentality that because you can't do everything, you can do nothing? How can this be combated?
- It's okay for our learning and receiving and hearing and seeing to outstrip our practice, as long as we are slowly adding to our practice. Remember, the turtle wins. What will you practice with intention and intensity over the next thirty days?

The Sad Truth behind So Many Rich People

41

PHILIPPIANS 4:10–12 | I rejoiced greatly in the Lord that at last you renewed your concern for me. Indeed, you were concerned, but you had no opportunity to show it. I am not saying this because I am in need, for I have learned to be content whatever the circumstances. I know what it is to be in need, and I know what it is to have plenty. I have learned the secret of being content in any and every situation, whether well fed or hungry, whether living in plenty or in want.

Consider This

There are two sets of values that live on two separate planes—one visible and the other invisible. On the visible plane we have wealth and poverty. On the invisible plane there is abundance and scarcity. A person can be financially wealthy yet be possessed by scarcity to such a degree that they might as well be in poverty. In other words, there are many rich people in the world (on the outside) who live like poor people (on the inside). To the contrary, there are many poor people in the world (on the outside) who live from an incredible place of abundance (on the inside). Wealth and poverty are the external, visible circumstances while scarcity and abundance are the internal, invisible realities. Paul gets this and gets at it in today's text.

The kingdom of this world is a kingdom of scarcity. The kingdom of heaven is a kingdom of abundance. Some of the wealthiest people I know live in the kingdom of scarcity. Paul shows us what living in the zone of the kingdom of abundance looks like.

I know what it is to be in need, and I know what it is to have plenty. I have learned the secret of being content in any and every situation, whether well fed or hungry, whether living in plenty or in want.

There is only one antidote to the cancer of scarcity: radical generosity. People of scarcity get richer and richer on the outside and more and more impoverished on the inside. It's why Jesus said it was so hard for a rich person to enter the kingdom of God (Matt. 19:23–24). This is why Jesus instructed the rich young ruler to sell everything he had and give the money to the poor and then come and follow him (Matt. 19:21). He knew the rich man's money had him. This is the sad and painful truth behind so many rich people. They aren't rich at all.

There's nothing so disheartening than to ask someone of great means for help and to be turned away. On the other hand, there's nothing quite so gratifying when someone who seemingly lacks the capacity to help you does so in a surprising way. This explains Paul's exuberant gratitude for the Philippians. Of all the churches he served, only the Philippians came through and helped him. Something tells me they were the least likely.

Abundance has nothing to do with how much or how little we have. We will get to the secret of this way of life tomorrow.

The Prayer

Abba Father, we thank you for your Son, Jesus, who is pure abundance wrapped in a cloak of scarcity. Thank you for the way he shows us how to find his abundance in the most unlikely places, even in the least of these. Fill us with the generosity of the Holy Spirit that we might give as you give. We pray in Jesus' name, amen.

The Questions

- Have you ever seen someone who appeared rich but who was actually a scarcity person? How about a person who appeared poor but who was an abundance person? Reflect on that.
- Are you an abundance person or a scarcity person?
- How can you grow as a person of abundance in the midst of plenty and in the midst of need?

42 The Problem with the Ultimate Bumper Sticker Scripture

PHILIPPIANS 4:12B–13 | I have learned the secret of being content in any and every situation, whether well fed or hungry, whether living in plenty or in want. I can do all this through him who gives me strength.

Consider This

If ever there were a verse of the Bible that screamed out, "Put me on a bumper sticker!" it is Philippians 4:13. We have mostly seen it in this framing: "I can do all things through Christ who strengthens me" (NKJV).

It's the favorite verse of athletes everywhere, those who won the state championship and those who didn't. It's the mantra of success-seekers in every industry. It's the Norman

Vincent Peale *Power of Positive Thinking* power verse. Yes, my friends, Philippians 4:13 is the ultimate I-think-I-can-Little-Engine-That-Could biblical secret sauce verse of all verses in the history of verses.

I don't want to rain on anyone's Super Bowl parade, but all of this is a gigantic adventure in missing the point of this text. It's a good moment to remember the words of Bible Jedi Knight Dr. Ben Witherington III (quoting D. A. Carson), who says, "A text without a context is merely a pretext for a proof-text" (i.e., whatever you want it to mean). Let's remember the context:

> I know what it is to be in need, and I know what it is to have plenty. I have learned the secret of being content in any and every situation, whether well fed or hungry, whether living in plenty or in want (v. 12).

The problem with our North American success approach is the emphasis on "I can do all things." Paul's emphasis decisively falls on "through Christ who strengthens me." Remember how Paul summed up his bio for the Galatians: "I have been crucified with Christ and I no longer live, but Christ lives in me" (Gal. 2:20a).

To be "crucified with Christ" means the "I can do all things" part of Philippians 4:13 takes on a decidedly different posture. It doesn't mean "I think I can." It means, rather, "I know I can't." It does not mean I can accomplish anything I set my mind to as long as Jesus is helping me. It means I can persevere and endure and, not only that, but thrive and overcome every obstacle thrown in the way of the gospel because I know the secret: Christ in me. It means a bank account flush with cash and an overdrawn checkbook are the same thing where Jesus is involved. Full or empty, plenty or in need, on top of the world or under the jail—they are all the same address because the address is Jesus.

The truth? I can't do all things through Christ who strengthens me. I can do all things he asks me to do and commands me to do and wants me to do because he lives in me, because "to live is Christ." I can make it through the darkest night and endure the hardest losses and suffer the gravest injustices—even to the point of losing my life— because "to die is gain" (Phil. 1:21). Jesus is my strength, and my life, and my all. He is "my rock, my fortress and my deliverer . . . my shield and the horn of my salvation, my stronghold" (Ps. 18:2). He is the secret to his own will being done on earth as it is in heaven.

Paul shows us what it looks like when a person unreservedly abandons themselves to Jesus. It is the rule, not the exception. The outcome, every single time someone does this, is glory to God.

The Prayer

Abba Father, we thank you for your Son, Jesus, who shows us what it looks like to live in the perfect union of love with you. Teach us this way of abandoning ourselves to Jesus in love. We have no hope of finding it lest you lead us. We want to be yours completely, come what may. We pray in Jesus' name, amen.

The Questions

- How do you relate to this pushback I am giving the cultural interpretation of Philippians 4:13?
- Do you see how the Christian faith gets pushed into self-improvement categories and even life-enhancement approaches? How is this a distraction to the essential message of the gospel?
- How do you relate to Paul's idea of contentment in today's text? Are plenty and want the same thing for you? How are you growing in this?

Why Most Giving Falls Short of True Giving

43

PHILIPPIANS 4:14–19 | Yet it was good of you to share in my troubles. Moreover, as you Philippians know, in the early days of your acquaintance with the gospel, when I set out from Macedonia, not one church shared with me in the matter of giving and receiving, except you only; for even when I was in Thessalonica, you sent me aid more than once when I was in need. Not that I desire your gifts; what I desire is that more be credited to your account. I have received full payment and have more than enough. I am amply supplied, now that I have received from Epaphroditus the gifts you sent. They are a fragrant offering, an acceptable sacrifice, pleasing to God. And my God will meet all your needs according to the riches of his glory in Christ Jesus.

Consider This

Outside of pure commerce, there are at least four basic frameworks for the exchange of money: investor/return, debtor/creditor, reciprocation, and giving. The first two are clear enough. An investor holds a stake in a business or venture and expects a return based on the company's profitability. A creditor lends money and expects to be repaid the money plus interest as a payment for the use of the money. Reciprocation is an arrangement where we return the favor on a more informal basis than a debtor/creditor relationship. It's more of a "I'll scratch your back, you scratch mine" relationship.

True giving is not just another category but another order of magnitude. Note, I said *true*. While all giving is good, most giving falls into one of the three other forms of exchange. We either expect to manage/control how our gift is stewarded/deployed, or we expect some kind of return from the recipient. That return can range anywhere from varying degrees of involvement in the direction of the venture as a stakeholder (investor), the ongoing management of a debt of gratitude and the varying forms of public recognition this takes (creditor), or the general unspoken but real expectation of returning the favor in kind (reciprocation).

I don't mean to eschew any of these approaches to giving as somehow inferior or wrong-minded. They can all be very helpful, beneficial to causes and organizations and used of God. They do not, however, rise to the level of true giving, or what giving means in the kingdom of God. True giving means giving to God with no expectation of return. True giving is a marker of real faith, because though we are giving to a person or organization we can see, we are doing it in a surrendered way that signals our deep mind and heart to a God we can't see. True giving is inspired by a hope not ruled by our expectations but born of the limitless possibilities of what God can do. Our expectations are to God's possibilities as a creditor's expectations are to a debtor's interest payment. Finally, true giving is infused with the freedom of love. When we know we have freely received love, we are empowered to freely give love.

To give from a surrendered place of faith, hope, and love rather than from a posture of expectation of return is a profound risk. We so often think of sacrificial giving as giving till it hurts or giving some percentage of our wealth we think we can't afford to give. I'm beginning to think that's just another worldly way of thinking about money.

True giving, which is to say sacrificial giving, cannot be measured in amounts, percentage or otherwise. It is the manifestation of a surrendered soul in love for God and others. When giving to God for others is done in this fashion, which cannot be faked, what comes back to the giver from God through others is so surprisingly extraordinary and so completely free that they wonder why they didn't give more. And they usually do. When people say things like, "You can't out give God," this is what they mean. They have entered into an economy that cannot be explained by mathematical accounting.

My best understanding is this is what Paul means in today's text when he says this to the Philippians concerning their giving:

They are a fragrant offering, an acceptable sacrifice, pleasing to God. And my God will meet all your needs according to the riches of his glory in Christ Jesus.

The Prayer

Abba Father, we thank you for your Son, Jesus, who is the giver and the gift and the ultimate vision of what giving even means. We are so bound by our expectations, be it for return on investment or our own self-interest or accruing the favor of others through doing favors for them. We want to give freely. Open our deepest soul to an ever deeper understanding that you have freely given us everything, and this will change everything. We pray in Jesus' name, amen.

The Questions

- Where are your sensibilities and sensitivities offended by today's writing?
- What is it about you that makes you susceptible to this particular kind of offense?
- How are you growing as a true and bona fide giver? Do you want to grow in this way? What will lead to more growth?

The Day Paul Dropped the Mic

44

PHILIPPIANS 4:20–22 | To our God and Father be glory for ever and ever. Amen.

Greet all God's people in Christ Jesus. The brothers and sisters who are with me send greetings. All God's people here send you greetings, especially those who belong to Caesar's household.

Consider This

Steve Jobs, the late founder and genius behind Apple and its remarkable run, patented a standard and yet always surprising way of closing out his keynote addresses. After giving updates on the stunning growth of the company, introducing a bevy of new products and software updates, and just when you thought it was all coming to a close, he would pause and with dramatic effect say, "But there is one more thing." After all the wowing updates and impressive new products, he always somehow managed to save the best for last, and we always loved it.

Paul runs this play in his closing to the letter to the Philippians. In the midst of standard sorts of closing words of greetings, he slips in something of an atomic bomb. It would not have been lost on the Philippians. After the updates on Epaphroditus's healing and his own soul's flourishing under the worst conditions, after giving them nugget after nugget of gospel gold, he almost nonchalantly delivers his "one more thing."

All God's people here send you greetings, especially those who belong to Caesar's household.

Hang on! Did Paul just say some of the villainous Emperor Nero's staff had become followers of Jesus Messiah! Yep, that's what he said. In the inner courts of the inner circle of the lordship of Caesar, there were brothers and sisters who staked their faith on the clarion creed "Jesus is Lord!" Wow! Talk about palace intrigue.

Especially those who belong to Caesar's household.

Paul, the prisoner, making disciples of everyone from the peasant servants to the Praetorian Guard. Paul, citizen of Rome, hidden away in a Roman jail where he would be sidelined—a threat to no one but perhaps a forgotten cellmate—infiltrates the emperor's household. How's that for a well-played "one more thing"? This is not the persuasion of Paul but the power of the gospel. Talk about an apostolic, epistolary mic drop! This is it!

Especially those who belong to Caesar's household.

Take that, Nero!

It reminds me of the story of Karol Wojtyla, a young Polish priest in the Roman Catholic Church in Krakow. In 1958 he served in a place called Nowa Huta, a new model Marxist city in Communist-occupied Poland. There was no church there. It was not allowed. Year after year after year, on Christmas Eve, he would lead the faithful out to an open field where they would secretly yet publicly celebrate the Mass, staking the cross of Christ in the ground of this bastion of godless Communism. Despite the short life expectancy of a priest in those days and times, he never flinched.

Twenty years later, in one of the stunning surprises of church history, against every expectation and defying all odds, the Polish priest Karol Wojtyla would be elected as the first Polish pope of the Roman Catholic Church. You know his papal name as Pope John Paul II. And just over a decade later, the Iron Curtain of Communism came crashing down.

This great gospel of the grace of God in Jesus Christ upends its enemies not by breaking down their doors but by infiltrating their minds and hearts with the love of God. There is no barrier that can ultimately withstand this gospel. On a certain unknown date in the future, either willingly or not, from Caesar's household to Caesar himself, every knee will bow and every tongue confess "that Jesus Christ is Lord, to the glory of God the Father" (Phil. 2:10–11)!

Fait accompli!

Especially those who belong to Caesar's household.

I'm dropping the mic now.

The Prayer

Abba Father, we thank you for your Son, Jesus, who overcomes through bowing down, who wins through losing, who is risen from the dead and who lives and reigns forevermore. So many speak of being on the right side of history. We want to be on the right side of the gospel. Come, Holy Spirit, and fill us with the mind of Christ and the very fullness of God. We pray in Jesus' name, amen.

The Questions

- Had you ever felt the drama of Paul's "one more thing" announcement of the greetings from Caesar's household? How about that!
- Do you really believe the gospel is God's comprehensive answer to sin and death and all the ways it has broken and breaks this world?
- Do you have an impossible story of the gospel's breakthrough in your life or know of one in another's life? Are you facing an impossible situation now? Is new faith rising up in you?

45 The Assumptions of Grace

PHILIPPIANS 4:23 | The grace of the Lord Jesus Christ be with your spirit. Amen.

Consider This

And so it ends as it began, by grace:

The grace of the Lord Jesus Christ be with your spirit. Amen.

I wish I better understood this little word we so readily throw around in the Christian faith. It has come to mean so much that it means almost nothing. I assume I know what it means, and so I just mouth the words and move on. I mean, I get it, right? You too?

Paul begins and ends every letter he writes with these same words, yet there is nothing standard about these kinds of greetings. He is not saying, "Hello again, hope you are well," or "Thanks for everything; wish you were here." He is not extending his own grace to us. He greets us with the very grace of the risen Lord Jesus Christ. The little word is loaded with assumptions, and, lest I regularly reexamine them, the word becomes little more than my own presumption.

So what does grace assume? Here goes. It assumes I know I am a sinner; that I was born a sinner; that I am a sinner, not because I sin, but that I sin because I am a sinner. Grace assumes I understand I am a son of Adam, infected with sin-cancer from the start, born with a terminal illness, and destined for destruction. I am, by nature, a child of wrath. It's not that God hates me; he loves me so much he will not allow me, a depraved sinner, to stand in his presence—for in his presence I am destroyed.

God is holy. This is his nature. Just as a fire consumes anything it is fed, so the holiness of God consumes whatever is not holy. And grace assumes I know that there is absolutely nothing I can do to make myself holy. Grace assumes that I understand that, apart from grace, I am hopeless. The holy God of the universe will not tolerate sin, not because he chooses not to but because he cannot, for to do so would be to deny his nature. The wrath of God is not an emotion but a simple fact of his existence.

Grace also assumes I know I am loved. I was loved at my birth, despite my sinful nature; loved every day of my life, despite my sin; and loved in and through my recalcitrant, rebellious resistance. Grace wants to make sure I know I am loved, not because of anything I have ever done or not done; nor am I not loved because of anything I have ever done or not done. Grace assumes I know I am loved because it is God's nature to love me.

Yes, grace assumes I know that God is holy and God is love and that these two eternal verities have been made known to us in this gospel: "For God so loved the world that he gave his one and only Son, that whoever believes in him shall not perish but have eternal life" (John 3:16).

Grace assumes I understand that "God demonstrates his own love for us in this: While we were still sinners, Christ died for us" (Rom. 5:8).

Grace assumes I get it that "God made him who had no sin to be sin for us, so that in him we might become the righteousness of God" (2 Cor. 5:21).

Grace is the unmerited, unmitigated favor of God for sinners like me and you. The more we recognize our sin, the more we recognize our need for God's grace; the more we recognize our need for God's grace, the more grace we are given; and the more grace we are given, the more we become the agents of his grace in the world for others.

When Paul says, "The grace of the Lord Jesus Christ be with your spirit. Amen," this is what he means.

The Prayer

Abba Father, we thank you for your Son, Jesus, who is grace and truth, holiness and love, God and man, giver and gift. Thank you for the cross where we find grace on grace on grace. Thank you. We pray in Jesus' name, amen.

The Questions

- Are you growing in your grasp of the grace of God in Jesus Christ?
- How has Paul's letter to the Philippians most encouraged you? Challenged you?
- What is your top takeaway from this letter and our journey through it?

THE SOWER'S CREED

Today,
I sow for a great awakening.

Today,
I stake everything on the promise of the Word of God.
I depend entirely on the power of the Holy Spirit.
I have the same mind in me that was in Christ Jesus.
Because Jesus is good news and Jesus is in me,
I am good news.

Today,
I will sow the extravagance of the gospel
everywhere I go and into everyone I meet.

Today,
I will love others as Jesus has loved me.

Today,
I will remember that the tiniest seeds become the
tallest trees; that the seeds of today become the shade
of tomorrow; that the faith of right now becomes
the future of the everlasting kingdom.

Today,
I sow for a great awakening.

9 781628 247992